The Allotment Planner

MORE THAN
200
WAYS TO ENJOY
YOUR PLOT
MONTH BY MONTH

The
Allotment
Planner

MORE THAN
200
WAYS TO ENJOY
YOUR PLOT
MONTH BY MONTH

Matthew
Appleby

INTRODUCTION BY
ALYS FOWLER

F
FRANCES LINCOLN LIMITED
PUBLISHERS

Frances Lincoln Limited
74–77 White Lion Street, London N1 9PF
www.franceslincoln.com

The Allotment Planner
Copyright © Frances Lincoln Limited 2013
Text copyright © Matthew Appleby 2013
Photographs copyright © see page 192

First Frances Lincoln edition 2013

A catalogue record for this book is available from
the British Library.

ISBN 978-0-7112-3470-3

Printed and bound in China

9 8 7 6 5 4 3 2 1

Contents

Introduction BY ALYS FOWLER

This book is an irreverent look at keeping an allotment. Despite all its tongue-in-cheek cynicism, there are very good ideas here because there's a lot more to a plot than whether it's been dug well. You need to fall in love with the space to return weekend after weekend. It's the silly, joyful, spontaneous activities that make it that kind of place. This book is here to remind you of that, so when the weeds won't go away or the slugs eat your hard work there is a reminder to throw a party, a recipe for building a bonfire and step-by-step instructions on how to dress a scarecrow.

I remember when Matthew first walked into the office. I was a features writer for *Horticulture Week*, a trade magazine about gardening, and Matt was to be the newshound. He wore a suit with pockets swollen from folded-over reporters' notebooks. I remember two distinct things from those days: that he liked to get into trouble, and then could do a wonderful sad-little-boy turn to get out of it, and that he liked cricket. There was no mention of gardening. Ever. There was a lot of cricket, though.

These days when we catch up there is very little cricket and lots of gardening. How times have changed! Mr Appleby has gone from a man who slept in a cupboard (really) to someone who spends his weekends digging with his children. I can't think of a better transformation.

Although I see that Matthew still likes getting into trouble. This book will push the realms of what an allotment can be – camping and peeing on your compost might be a step too far for some. Still, I love turning a plot into more than just a place to go and garden: inviting friends over for a lunchtime barbeque that runs into the evening is one of the joys of having such a space.

I believe there's much to be said for making the plot a destination for the whole day rather than for a few stolen hours. Part of achieving that is including the whole family – building sandpits, slides and places to sit and enjoy a glass or two in the evening sun. And if it does get too much, before you start getting angry letters from the management about weeds, think about plot-sharing. It works brilliantly, whether it's a long-term thing or just for a season. It turns the whole act of gardening into something truly sociable. It's amazing how much you can get done with many hands.

There is plenty in here to inspire. Just don't – whatever you do – leave this book at home: it's one to sit in the allotment shed, to jot notes in and, when it's sheeting down with rain, to read and dream of how to celebrate warmer days to come.

January

'Keep love in your heart. A life
without it is like a sunless garden
when the flowers are dead.
The consciousness of loving and
being loved brings a warmth
and richness to life that nothing
else can bring.'

Oscar Wilde, *A Woman of No Importance*

Allotment scene by acrylic artist Chris Cyprus.

THREE IDEAS: ARTISTIC LICENCE

❶ **Make your plot a sculpture park** – gnomes are gardeners' sculptures of choice, but you can be more tasteful.

❷ **Apply outdoor art** such as murals and mosaics to the fences and shed walls.

❸ **Make land sculpture** from stones, soil, sticks, grass (mown-in designs) or pave a patch for chalk drawings.

Picture the scene

Early photos of a newly acquired plot may include head-high brambles, dumped shopping trolleys and other unwelcome ornaments. If you take over a messy plot, make sure you take pictures of the scene before you start to clear it, because you are unlikely to put this stuff back afterwards and you will rue the missed photo opportunity for 'before' and 'after' comparisons. During the winter, if you miss your plot and want to reconnect with the magic, dig out the photos and start drawing from them. It is better, but more difficult, to paint on site and in the open air, but painting from snaps is a good way to start.

How to get started

Do not start with paint unless you are experienced. Use charcoal for preparatory sketches. It frees up your drawing so you are not producing tiny etches. Use good swings of the arm on large pieces of paper and rub in the charcoal to create shaded parts, using your thumb and forefinger. For perspective, hold out your charcoal at arm's length and measure the size of something with one eye shut. Translate that to the page. Maybe double or treble each measurement to fill the paper. Allotments can be quite brown and green. Uniform raised beds and superstore sheds do not improve the view, but flowers, random pieces of painted wood and – most of all – people help to add colour. For inspiration, look at Van Gogh's *Sunflowers* or that Dutch artist's *Potato Eaters* paintings. Take photos of interesting allotment neighbours (or ask them to pose), or of cheeky kids to populate your pictures.

Chris Cyprus, from Mossley near Manchester, was a carpet fitter who painted as a hobby before contracting cancer, recovering and taking up a unique career painting allotment scenes. He uses acrylics, which dry more quickly than oils, and can be painted on top of each other straight from the tube. His pictures feature bold outlines. This works well for allotments because you can ensure the beds and the crops look distinct, rather than having the greens and browns merge. Another simple medium is coloured pastels. Cartooning with pens is simple. Watercolours and oils are more complex to work with.

For photographing your plot, think of more unusual views: snowy plots, misty early mornings, photos taken from high up or low down, or even extreme close-ups. Take regular snaps and use them not only so you can picture your plot more easily at home, but also as a record of the ups and downs of your allotment adventure.

Art equipment required: charcoal; A3/A2 paper; board and masking tape; acrylic paint; thick brushes. Also try www.rhs.org.uk/competitions/photo-competition. See Chris Cyprus's work at www.allotmentart.com.

January

....

....

....

....

Time to sow . . .

INDOORS

- broad beans ● lettuce ● onions
- peas ● radish ● salad onions

UNDER GLASS

- strawberries

Time to chit . . .

INDOORS

- potatoes

....

....

....

....

....

....

....

....

....

....

....

....

....

....

....

....

....

Time to harvest . . .

- Brussels sprouts • leeks
- parsnips • swedes • turnips
- winter cabbage

Time to force . . .

- rhubarb (by covering with a pot)

'Nothing is more completely the child of art than a garden.'

Sir Walter Scott, *On Ornamental Plantations and Landscape Gardening*

Join the committee

Volunteering for the allotment committee is a dangerous game if you do not have much time or patience, but it can be rewarding. The committee's duties may include collecting the rent, organising social events, inspecting plots and running sales. If you want to get involved – or if you have accounting, organisational or party planning skills to offer – then go for it. If you hate committees and long meetings, steer clear.

If you are on the committee, you can become one of the 'allotment police' and inspect fellow allotment holders' plots. The chances are that yours will be viewed a bit more favourably too, particularly if it is a little unkempt.

The need to patrol allotments arises from the fact that some new plot-holders are turning their backs on their plots, perhaps falling out of love with 'grow your own' because of the hard work, bad weather and sometimes disappointing returns. Recently, Merton Council in London issued 'dirty plot' notices to almost a third of its plots in eighteen months, that is 378 notices to quit on 1,364 plots!

So there is plenty of work to be done on allotment committees. Inspections, evictions, events and rent collecting cover most of it, but looking after the shop could be an option too.

Rents and legal issues

The legal side of allotments is a minefield, but could be of interest too. National surveys need to be carried out regularly to monitor where allotments are being lost to building, how long waiting lists are and how much plot-holders pay in rent. This could be for you.

Some allotment committees have exciting ideas about becoming self-sustaining in water and electricity (by collecting run-off rainwater from sheds and other roofs and by using solar panels). Some plan to make cash from opening a shop or renting space to Christmas-tree sellers and beekeepers. You could get involved.

Most of all, a long winter without gardening can be lonely, and getting to know like-minded people and mulling over ideas on how to make your plot work better can be fun.

THREE IDEAS: ALLOTMENT AUTHORITY

❶ **Join an area allotment committee** advising councils or national allotment groups. See National Allotment Society website: www.nsalg.org.uk.

❷ **An eviction notice** received is not something to boast about, but will quickly recharge your interest and ensure you know the workings of the committee.

❸ **Declare your plot a free state**, with its own flag and constitution, as a temporary solution.

16

THREE IDEAS: RAISING YOUR PROFILE

❶ **Try to get on the radio** or in local paper with your allotment tips. Just call the editor and sell yourself.

❷ **Contribute to other blogs** – some garden bloggers and garden companies send daily bulletins in which they collect other bloggers' pieces. Make like-minded friends through LinkedIn, Facebook and Twitter and spread your word by getting them to forward to their followers what you are saying.

❸ **Write an allotment book**, such as a year on an allotment picture book through www.albelli.co.uk/products/photo-books.

Share your plot with the world

Allotments make fertile ground for bloggers. The blogosphere is a good place to share and celebrate achievements, and it fulfils the need for support and advice. Garden bloggers often meet up at flower shows and love commenting on each other's blogs and tweets. Twitter is the ideal way to announce your blog to the world and interact with fellow bloggers and enthusiasts. Ideally, you want your blog to appear where interested people are already surfing: horticulture businesses might enjoy your fresh musings on their website, or garden publications might welcome your insights on their home pages. Gardeners like to share things from their gardens, even their thoughts: it is a great way to learn and be inspired.

Get started

Use your blog to join an allotment community. If you use the hashtag '#allotment' on Twitter and describe yourself as an allotment lover, tweeting relentlessly, replying to anyone who mentions 'allotments', before you know it you will attract hundreds of followers. To join in the conversation, get on to allotment chat sites such as http://chat.allotment.org.uk. They will offer plenty of tips and banter. Retweet any good tweets and you will become friends for life with the tweeter you are promoting.

Some bloggers now write daily newsletters and a few have graduated to paid writing. If you are tweeting or blogging from an event such as the RHS Chelsea Flower Show, the wider media might pick up on what you write if it is interesting enough. Use Instagram (http://instagram.com/developer/register/) to share photos of what you are doing and any interesting things you might see.

A large part of allotment blogging is finding something worth saying. Ask yourself: would you write home about this? Is this worth sharing, or am I better off just writing a diary for myself?

Build your own blog at http://wordpress.com. Join microblogging site Twitter (with its maximum 140-character messages) at https://twitter.com/signup. Think of a username and password, add a picture of yourself, follow people and fill in your biography. Download TweetDeck and add topics you want to monitor through the site.

The secret of Twitter is getting your thoughts retweeted by other users in order to reach the biggest audience. To do this, do not be boring. If you attract a lot of followers (more than 3,000), do not get arrogant, but use Twitter to communicate with celebrities. Give them career feedback.

Start trends such as guerrilla garlanding (see page 184), or look after your business and build a brand for yourself. Tweet breaking news; do not talk about the weather or be smug. As you make allotment friends, avoid forming a clique – always remember that other people are watching.

January

....

....

....

....

....

....

....

....

....

....

....

....

....

....

....

....

....

....

....

....

....

'I am writing in the garden. To write as one should of a garden one must write not outside it or merely somewhere near it, but in the garden.'

Frances Hodgson Burnett, *The Secret Garden*

....

....

....

....

....

....

....

....

....

....

....

....

....

....

Walk on the wild side

Wild flowers are enjoying a golden moment: UK sales of cornflowers (*Centaurea cyanus*), field poppies (*Papaver rhoeas*) and other wispy natives tripled in 2012, and the wildflower meadows at the Olympic Park in Stratford, East London set a good example of how such landscapes work. These ten 'football fields' of wildflower meadows were carefully planned and sown to reach their peak in time for the arrival of the torches in July and sported an 'Olympic gold' colour scheme throughout August. Even on a much smaller scale, the benefits of wild flowers are simple: the wildlife you attract, the visual interest and the fantastic movement. Mini-meadows contain nectar-rich annual and perennial wildflower mixes, such as pot marigolds (*Calendula officinalis*), tickseed (*Coreopsis tinctoria*) and hybrids of corn marigold (*Glebionis segetum*).

Get the look

To get the meadow look, you do not have to convert it all into a wildflower sanctuary. Start with a small, manageable area of 4 x 4m (12 x 12ft).

The two times to sow are March and September. On lighter soils, autumn-sown seed generally germinate and establish quickly, although some will not come up until the following spring. But you can get started by planting wildflower plug plants at any time of the year (from www.wigglywigglers.co.uk or http://meadowmania.co.uk), or by buying a wildflower meadowmat by the square metre (www.meadowmat.com).

Next, research which seed mix to use to fill in around the plug plants. Some combine perennials and annuals; while others sow annuals only; there are mixes for sunny spots or shade. Try Nova-Flore meadow seed mixes (www.meadowinmygarden.co.uk), Wiggly Wigglers grassy or flower meadow mix, or use a meadow-flower seed mix from Pictorial Meadows (www.pictorialmeadows.co.uk).

Do not think you can just throw wildflower seed on to grass and transform it into a meadow. You may get some germination, but if you want it to look like the pretty picture on the box, turn over the soil so it is not compacted, remove weeds and make sure the seed is watered.

If you want to convert a grass area, strip away the top layer of lawn turf. Dig out 10cm (4in) of soil below the layer of grass to reduce the soil fertility and the germination of weed seeds.

> ### THREE IDEAS: FURTHER WILDNESS
>
> **1** Roll out some wildflower turf for an instant meadow.
>
> **2** Are you a lazy gardener who wants to grow flowers from a bottle at the shake of a wrist? **You can buy flower shakers** that include flower seed and fertilizer in coir for quick and easy sowing.
>
> **3** Have a go at guerrilla gardening by broadcasting wildflower seed on wasteland.

emove any turf with a spade and set
ide to reuse as compost when rotted.

2. Prepare the soil by turning it over to
   reduce compaction and remove weeds.

PLANT A WILDFLOWER AREA: STEP BY STEP

w seed by hand and water it in
refully to assist germination.

4. Wild flowers in bloom make an
   eye-catching spectacle.

February

'… beauty is a by-product.
The main business of
gardens is sex and death.'
Sam Llewellyn, on his novel *The Sea Garden*

THREE IDEAS: BEES IN YOUR BONNET

1 **Sell your honey** and harvest your honeycomb. Try farmers' markets, fetes or sell from the garden gate by sticking up a sign saying 'Knock: fresh home-produced honey for sale'. Or join the Women's Institute and sell through one of their sales.

2 **Go on a beekeeping course** or teach others how to keep bees once you have the knowledge.

3 Try www.dragonfli.co.uk for a **Beepol box of bumblebees** to get you started with pollinators.

Create your own buzz

At first glance, an allotment seems like the perfect place to keep bees. The hives are surrounded by lots of pollen and honey-producing nectar from the crops, and city sites, which are often fenced and locked, are relatively safe havens. Those in favour like the idea of bees pollinating their plants, and bees are under threat from pesticides, the *Varroa* mite and loss of habitat, so getting a hive is good for the environment. Those against think that the bees might be dangerous and that the space would be better used for growing.

Getting started

Beekeeping on your plot may be a non-starter if your allotment committee is opposed. Bear in mind there will be rules to police you. Keeping bees needs only a minimum of half an hour per week with a hive. The bees mostly look after themselves and will not notice if you go on holiday. Urban allotments are often better for bees than the countryside with its monoculture crops. Think about planting daffodils, cherries, blackcurrants, rosemary, thyme, fennel, sweet peas, cardoons, heather, lavender, cornflowers and foxgloves to provide year-round nectar.

Let your neighbours know. Buy locally bred, well-behaved bees from a reputable supplier. Ask other beekeepers to help. They may have bees for sale too. Early in the year you will be able to buy a six-frame nucleus of bees with brood, food and the essential queen.

Ensure the entrance of the hive does not point into a footpath or busy area so their flight paths do not impinge on your neighbours' enjoyment of their allotments. Take a beginners' course with the British Beekeepers Association (www.bbka. org.uk). You will need clothing, tools (including a bee-smoker to calm bees) and (obviously) a hive. Do not handle bees when other people are close.

One risk is allowing the strength of colonies to increase to swarming strength in an unmanaged way. Avoid this by seeking expert advice on dividing the colony, clipping the wings of the queen bee, re-queening, 'shook swarm technique' (shaking of the worker bees, together with the queen, into a clean, empty hive) and avoiding overcrowding. It may be best to put your hive in a remote area of the allotment. Make sure the bees rise 1.8m (6ft) or more before leaving the plot by use of screening, such as natural hedging, fencing or fine-mesh screening. Ensure the flight path (of low-flying bees) is not directly across other plots. Have a mate around, in case of emergencies, which might include being stung more than once.

First-year beekeepers usually get only a small harvest of honey by late summer as the colony builds up. Check every two weeks in summer to see if frames are filled with wax-capped honey, then harvest them when they are mostly full.

February

....

....

....

....

....

Time to sow . . .

UNDER CLOCHES

(on soil that has been covered to warm it)

- beetroot • broad beans • lettuce
- onions • peas • radish
- salad onions • spinach
- summer cabbage

Time to chit . . .

INDOORS

- potatoes

....

....

....

....

....

....

....

....

....

....

....

....

....

....

....

....

....

28

Time to plant . . .

- bare-root fruit trees and bushes
- fruit canes • Jerusalem artichokes
- shallots

Time to harvest . . .

- Brussels sprouts • kale • leeks
- parsnips • purple-sprouting
broccoli • salsify • scorzonera
- swedes • turnips

'Gardening is the art that uses flowers
and plants as the paint and the soil and
sky as the canvas'

Elizabeth Murray, *Monet's Passion*

Keep chickens, hens, ducks and geese

Chicken sales have rocketed in recent years as the return to the good life during the recession became more attractive. The lure of cheap and healthy eggs and meat, plus the enjoyment of having a truly useful and idiosyncratic pet, has attracted good-lifers to the pastime. Some say chickens make a house a home. And there is something magical about finding a warm egg and eating it. You can guarantee that the chickens are well reared and do not have to worry about battery farming or use of antibiotics or hormones in your birds. Saving cash is possible, as is improving your own health by eating healthy, fresh eggs and poultry. You can also use chicken manure to fertilize the garden. If you believe you are raising a better product, the financial gains are not so important.

Getting started

You will need a coop and a water dispenser, as well as chicken food and a feeder. Buy an Eglu (www.omlet.co.uk/shop/eglu) if you are feeling rich, select a wooden coop on a mid-price budget or build your own. You will need basic carpentry skills and tools. Chickens need a nest box, pop hole, roof, perches and a floor to their coop. Three chickens is a good break-even number. You might buy free-range, but bought products that include egg, such as cakes, are very likely to be from Europe's 'yellow river' of non-free-range egg production. Home-kept chickens might be better fed than farmed birds, so will produce healthier eggs. Chickens prefer grass or wood chips and need 0.4 sq.m (4ft 4in) per bird, with an outdoor run of about the same size.

You will need a fence to guard against foxes, which normally get in through a small hole under a gate or fence. Use poultry fencing or an electric fence or electric poultry netting. A non-electric fence should be 2.2m (7ft) high and have an outward-sloping top to stop a hungry fox from climbing over.

Vaccination is essential to guard against spreading illnesses such as Marek's disease, Avian flu, Newcastle disease and infectious bronchitis. Be careful to observe hygiene. Chickens are reported as causing children (who usually love them) to get diarrhoea.

Prices are from 50p for an ex-battery bird to £30 for garden-centre top breeds. They might last three years. Food costs maybe £15 a year. But in an ideal 'permaculture' world, you would feed chickens only (free) household scraps and plot pests. Expect more than 200 eggs a year, with more in the summer. You will need a chicken sitter if you want to go away. Maybe there are opportunities for professional services setting up to look after holidaying chicken-owners' flocks.

Chickens can be food or friends on your plot.

THREE IDEAS: FEATHERED FRIENDS

❶ **Keep fancy breeds** for show: ducks, geese, quails (or even pigs, if you are allowed) are interesting alternatives to chickens.

❷ **Sell eggs and chickens:** eggs last four weeks after being laid and you need to give them a 'best before' date by law. Try farmers' markets or sell from the garden gate. Make a sign to advertise eggs from your own chickens: you can turn it over to say 'sold out', which shows they are fresh.

❸ If you fancy a carpentry project **make your own chicken run.**

1. Add green waste to the compost heap and turn regularly to promote rotting.

2. Once the waste is thoroughly rotted, move the new compost to beds for cr

FEED YOUR SOIL: STEP BY STEP

3. Dig in the new compost and leave for a couple of months before planting.

4. Reap the rewards with well-fed crops such as these healthy aubergines.

Supercharge your soil

Fertilizing your plot is essential to feed your crops, but does not take any gardening skill, or even much interest in horticulture. At a very basic level, you can urinate on your plot – the nitrogen is great for the plants. You can encourage your kids to do it too, especially on the raspberries and in the compost. You could go further and use human excrement. Use your own manure, placed in a bucket and covered in sawdust, to add to the compost heap and, when rotted with the usual veg scraps and so on, you have got something out of nothing.

Getting started

One of the more conventional ways of adding essential food to your soil is by green manuring. Green manures are fast-growing plants broadcast sown to cover soil. When grown, chop down and roughly dig in, to a depth of 25cm (10in), two weeks before spring planting, to fix nitrogen harvested from the air into the soil and improve soil structure. Sow in autumn and dig in the next spring. Your plot will not be doing anything else and to eke out the last nutrients before they are washed away by winter rains is a good thing. Watch out for allotment 'police', who might think that you have a weedy, overgrown plot.

Green manures are usually sown in late summer or autumn and mop up any nutrients, preventing them being washed away by winter rain. Hardy winter grazing rye and winter tares grow all winter. You can buy green manures from most seed companies.

Alfalfa should be sown April to July and is good for alkaline soils.

Bitter blue lupin suits light, sandy, acid soils. Sow March to June.

Crimson clover is good for light soils. Sow March to August.

Mustard is sown from March to September.

Buckwheat is sown in spring and prevents the spread of weeds.

Well-rotted animal manure from horses, cattle, pigs, sheep, chickens, turkeys, rabbits, humans and guano from seabirds and bats all are useful soil nutrients. Animal manure improves the soil structure so that it holds more nutrients and water. It also encourages soil microbial activity, which promotes the soil's trace mineral supply. Animal manure also contains some nitrogen and other nutrients that help the growth of plants.

Horse manure is most common and is often available free (with delivery) from stables. It is full of weed seeds and straw, though. A rare risk is that the horse manure could be contaminated with pesticides from the grass the horse eats, and these might kill your crops. Sheep manure is high in nitrogen and potash, and chicken litter is good for nitrogen and protein.

Clay soils, which get sticky in rain and crusty when dry, can benefit from manuring, as well as adding grit and sand. Chalky soils, which can lack nutrients and can dry easily, do better with the addition of green manures. Spent mushroom compost is also a useful soil conditioner.

February

'Well, I don't use the toilet much to pee in. I almost always pee in the yard or the garden, because I like to pee on my estate.'

Iggy Pop, quoted by Erik Hedegaard, *Rolling Stone* magazine

THREE IDEAS: FERTILE GROUND

❶ **Seaweed**: collect from the beach and use as a mulch to keep down weeds, add minerals to the soil, retain moisture and repel slugs.

❷ **Bark and woodchips**: spread on surface to retain water over presoaked soil between established plants in early spring. Alternatives are coir (coconut fibre) soil conditioner, Strulch mineralised straw mulch and biochar (charcoal that increases soil fertility and is environmentally sound).

❸ **Rock dust**: this is a rock powder containing minerals and trace elements, and is used in organic farming as it helps soil fertility, structure and drainage.

February

Go green

If you really want to put something back into the environment rather than taking from the earth, think seriously about greening your plot. That does not just mean installing a water butt to harvest rainwater from the shed roof; it entails not using pesticides, peat, non-organic fertilizers, plastics or mains water.

Do not drive to your allotment – bike or walk instead. Using petrol and causing pollution ruins the environmental aim of growing your own. Use a wheelbarrow to cart heavy items to the plot, and campaign to dig up the car park and make it into another plot. Use a garden centre local enough that you do not have to drive – or request delivery.

Positive steps to carbon neutrality can include installing a solar panel on your shed roof. A solar panel is unlikely to be economically advantageous, but you have to weigh up the pros of being green with the cons of it not always saving you cash.

Gardeners can be complacent, believing that just because they grow plants they are environmentally positive. Those plants release oxygen and eat CO_2, and can be eaten so you do not have to buy them, which cuts transport emissions. But, for instance, a garden-centre business sells lots of plants but cannot hope to be carbon neutral because most of its customers drive to it.

A pet cemetery puts nutrients back into the soil rather than using energy at the crematorium. A ground source heat pump uses the warmth of the earth to create power. Hang out your washing rather than using a tumble dryer. Be wary of buying stone, timber and concrete, all of which have environmental impacts. Avoid using the precious resources of oil or gas in items such as heat lamps, patio heaters and barbecues or when mowing. Use sustainable charcoal, locally grown plants, reclaimed timber and recovered bricks.

Get the look

A greener alternative to using man-made fences or walls is to make earth-rammed walls of clay. Compress a damp mixture of earth that has suitable proportions of sand, gravel and clay into a clamped wooden frame or mould, to create either a solid wall of earth or individual blocks. Add lime or animal blood to stabilize the material. Pour in damp material to a depth of 10–25cm (4–10in) and then compact with a hand tamper to half its original height. The walls become too hard to work after about an hour.

There are many ways to make your gardening greener.

THREE IDEAS: GREENER OPTIONS

❶ Hoe often rather than use weedkiller. Plant densely and use a no-dig method to avoid bringing weed seeds to the top. Cut out chemicals and use animal and green manure. Make compost using food and garden waste.

❷ Create habitats for wildlife by leaving wild patches for bee-friendly plants such as poppies, lavender and sunflowers, and encourage birds with feeders and by planting berrying plants.

❸ Go vegan: there is no better way to save the planet. It takes at least three times as much water to grow food to feed a meat-eater than it does to feed a vegan. Vegan diets also produce fewer greenhouse-gas emissions than meat-based diets.

March

'If you have a garden and a library,
you have everything you need.'

Marcus Tullius Cicero to Varro,
Letters: To My Friends, IX, iv

Try your hand at topiary

You do not have to buy an expensive box tree to take up the art of topiary. The chances are you already have a shrub or tree that you can prune on your plot. But while pruning is utilitarian, topiary is art, and a good example of this are the gardens of Levens Hall in Cumbria, with its artful and ancient, topiarized hedging.

The appeal of the clipped box is that it is formal and looks impressive, while being easy to maintain. All you need to do is to buy a pair of shears to keep the topiary bush neatly trimmed all year round. Topiary adds individuality to your plot and, if you operate on a Levens Hall-style scale, you can create a distinctive screen. Creating topiary is addictive. Plants for topiarizing need to be dense, small-leaved, and have flexible, young shoots that recover quickly from clipping. Yew, privet, bay, rosemary, lavender, holly and Leylandii are all good in a container or in a border. Box is liable to get unsightly blight and may be best avoided. Almost any woody plant that can be clipped into a hedge works as topiary. A whole hedge with a run of shapes along the top looks great.

Get the look

The key to successful topiary is using a frame to cut around, but you can make your own frame using chicken wire in any shape you like.

Start by gently placing the frame over your selected tree or bush. Push the branches through the wires. Trim the branches at the point where they stick out of the wiring. Trim and prune the branches back to the wiring regularly so that the shrub begins to grow around the frame. Prune from June onwards, when leaves are tougher, or in spring when bruised leaves are quickly hidden by new growth.

It is risky to make shapes by eye so use a garden cane as a cutting guide for straight edges or make a template from cardboard.

To make topiary balls, twist garden wire into a circle slightly smaller than your bush. Move the twisted wire over the plant as you prune.

Topiary is art and it is easy to maintain.

For cones, make a wigwam of three canes around a bush; wrap wire round the lot. Use your shears to prune on the framework.

THREE IDEAS: PERFECTLY PRUNED

❶ **Plant a maize maze**, or even a hedge maze (which is a longer-term project).

❷ **Make a turf labyrinth** or maze, by cutting a convoluted path into grass; cut a turf tattoo by killing areas of grass to 'etch' a shape in the turf; or cover turf with a stencil, so that the grass yellows and shows up against the green.

❸ **Create false topiary** by growing ivy up topiary frames, then wiring the ivy in and clipping it to shape.

March

Time to sow . . .

INDOORS
- cauliflowers • globe artichokes
- lettuce • peppers • tomatoes

UNDER GLASS
- sow aubergines

DIRECT IN THE PLOT
- herbs • carrots

Time to plant . . .

- asparagus crowns • bare-root
fruit trees and bushes • beetroot
- broad beans • cabbage • onion
sets • parsnips • peas • potatoes
- salads • spinach • turnips
- young veg plants

'Plant carrots in January and
you'll never have to eat carrots.'

Anon

Time to harvest . . .

- chards • leeks • parsnips
- spinach beet

Grow giant vegetables

Growing large veg for competition is predominantly a male pursuit. Giant crops do not taste as good as smaller crops, but they get the Olympic juices going. The most important factor is choosing the right seed, and the internet is a good place to find it. Type 'big pumpkin seed' for instance into a search engine to give you some options.

There is a magic in creating veg of *Jack and the Beanstalk* proportions. The produce might taste watery or woody, but who cares if you get your red rosette and your picture in the newspaper.

How to do it

Growing giant fruit and veg takes some considerable gardening skill. Buy seed that will produce enormous specimens, and use the full growing season. Start the seed in a greenhouse before spring, add water and nutrients and hope for sunshine.

Dig deeply and spread manure in the autumn before planting. Test the soil using kits for the three major nutrients – nitrogen (N), phosphorus (P) and potassium (K) – and for soil pH level and replenish any nutrients that might be lacking. Add slow-acting organic fertilizers at planting time.

Leafy veg, such as cabbage, require high nitrogen. Add before planting or topdress when your crop is growing.

Phosphorus is good for seed germination and root development, and extra doses are essential for roots such as carrots.

Plants grown for their fruit, such as pumpkins and tomatoes, need a fertilizer that is high in potassium (sometimes called potash) and phosphorus. High-potash tomato feed is a favourite. You will also need to add sulphate of ammonia to the soil.

Regular heavy waterings are essential to ensure growth and no splitting of the fruit or veg. You must thin the runts of the litter so the few remaining giants can dominate. Later on, concentrate on only the potential champion. Be on pest and disease watch and pick off pests. Diseases may be more problematic and need treating at once.

More tips: water with compost tea. Save seed from the largest vegetables you grew the previous year. Place protective straw or a mat under a giant vegetable to stop it rotting. Do not grow the same plant in the same place the next year to avoid disease build-up.

> ## THREE IDEAS: COMPETITIVE SPIRIT
>
> ❶ **Auction your giant crops** for charity on the internet or at your allotment show.
>
> ❷ **Cook up your monster** and serve to gardening friends to eat at the gardening show or at your allotment dinner.
>
> ❸ Look at the other categories in the garden shows and enter them too. The **UK Giant Vegetable Competition** takes place at the Malvern Autumn Show.

1. ...epare the ground for sowing pumpkins. ...e seed from previous year's champions.

2. Water and feed the plants regularly. A high-potash tomato food benefits growth.

CULTIVATE A CHAMPION: STEP BY STEP

3. ...arvest the pumpkins when their skins ...ve been ripened by the sun.

4. Protect the skins of giant pumpkins when moving them and give them a soft bed.

1st Place

THREE IDEAS: MAKING A LIVING

❶ **Organize a plant fair** on your plot (with permission) and charge rent. Sell your plants, eggs, honey and other produce at the fair or from a market stall.

❷ **Hire out/sublet your plot**, if allowed, for car parking, to film companies, as a campsite or as a plot share.

❸ Get hold of a metal detector and use it to find the right place to **dig for treasure** (check out the rules first).

Earn money from your plot

Grow to sell: there is nothing that gets my juices bubbling more than the idea of making money. The outlay to start your own gardening business is small, especially if you have an allotment. Growing veg to be self-sufficient with some left to sell could be viable and is good for your own food security (not having to rely on others for food). For 99 per cent of us it is always going to be much cheaper to buy commercially grown food from the shops. To suggest otherwise is an insult to professional growers.

But if you are good at growing there is a chance to make some cash and, even if you are not, there might be. Strawberry and tomato plants sell best at car boot sales, farmers' markets and fetes. Check supermarket shelves and identify which crops cost most. Grow these in abundance and sell the surplus. The average UK rent for a plot is relatively cheap compared to most hobbies, so anything you make over this is profit.

How to do it

Garlic is easy to grow. You just plant a clove in winter and sell a bulb in the spring. However, you need to raise some seedlings to make money from most plants. The trick is to grow plants that are expensive to buy, which excludes potatoes and cabbage. Unusual tomatoes, berries and herbs are better.

You will need seed compost, seed, seed trays, a greenhouse, a conservatory or a propagator. Do a deal with your local garden centre to buy the pots that they would usually throw away; get them for a discounted price or for free. Many garden centres collect old pots as a service but have no use for them.

Pursue several paths to market by selling 'retail' at car boot sales and to friends and neighbours, and selling 'wholesale' at local garages and shops. Or leave potted plants outside your front gate and trust passers-by to put money in the honesty box when they remove a plant.

If you do have a horticulture certificate (for instance from the Royal Horticultural Society), that will help you if you want to garden for other people. This does not require a plot, although having an allotment can be useful as a place to dump and burn waste collected during your work. Garden for friends, or seek work by word of mouth. A note in the newsagent's window is good. For your services, charge £10–20 an hour, depending on the affluence of your area. You will need transport and tools. Busy people with gardens usually want tidy-ups doing. So a lawnmower, strimmer, hedgetrimmer and possibly a chainsaw are good to have with you. You may be expected to take away the trimmings. Say you want to visit regularly – weekly or monthly – and set up a contract so you get regular cash year round.

March

'The physician can bury his mistakes, but the architect can only advise his client to plant vines.'

Frank Lloyd Wright, *The New York Times*

Grow your own wine

Grapes and wine are both symbols of the good life. Many people have happy memories of vineyards visited on holiday. Vague memories, but happy ones. Growing grapes can add interest to your plot. And you can expect to produce table grapes (if grown in a greenhouse, because they need more warmth to get sweet enough to eat raw) and even, perhaps, make your own wine.

How to plant vines

Growing decent grapes is difficult and takes horticultural skill. You will require a sunny fence. Plant in autumn or spring.

You need to support the vines with horizontal galvanized wires, 30cm (12in) apart, stretched and attached to vine eyes (long, metal supports bent at one end to form an hole to run the wire through); the vine eyes are fixed to the wall using a drill. If you are not growing next to a fence or wall, attach the wires to posts.

In sandy or stony soil, dig a hole 15cm (6in) away from your fence or wall. Make sure the hole is bigger than the root ball of the vine. Add manure and grit into the hole. Space plants 1.5m (5ft) apart.

Pruning is the hardest and most complicated part. In winter of year one, prune the new vine to within two buds of the bottom. When buds come out in spring, remove the top bud leaving the remaining one to grow, tied to the wires vertically. Chop out all side shoots on the vine.

In spring of year two let three side shoots grow, then in autumn chop the top stem to three buds and train the other two shoots to either side and tie to horizontal wires.

In year three train the side shoots vertically to the wires and hope they bear fruit. Feed with potash to help. After harvest, cut the two branches back to the main stem. Then cut the new centre shoot back to three buds and tie in the two side shoots to replace the branches that have fruited.

If the crop fails, at least you get nice leaf colour in the autumn.

THREE IDEAS: VINTAGE CROPS

❶ **Make your own wine:** Chateau Allotment 2012 has a nice ring to it. Or use grape concentrates if your crop fails from www.homewinemaking.co.uk.

❷ **Visit vineyards** to get inspired to grow your own grapes.

❸ **Sell your grapes** to a communal press and contribute to your community wine vintage, or set up your own communal press if there is not one locally.

THREE IDEAS: SUNFLOWER SUCCESS

❶ Harvest sunflower oil from the sunflower seeds. Blend the seeds, roast at 150°C (300°F), press in a garlic press and strain and cool. Consume what little you produce within two weeks. Better still, buy a seed press/oil extractor and grind the seeds – this works quite efficiently.

❷ Arrange them as cut flowers: the cut-your-own trend has threatened to take over from grow-your-own in recent years.

❸ Dry seeds for eating: cut off the sunflower heads in autumn. Rub off the seeds and bake them for three hours at 93°C (200°F). Salt to taste.

Aim high with sunflowers

Kids love growing sunflower, as do adults, who can get competitive with it. Sunflowers are beautiful too. Watching them shoot up from seed in the ground to above your head is exciting even for a grown-up. The allotment competition might be for the tallest plant, or for the biggest seed head, so the entries can be judged in a room alongside the prize tomatoes and jars of jam topped with gingham and greaseproof paper.

Fading giants become as special as pets. Collect their seed at the end of the year so you are ready for the next growing season. Get your children to adopt one sunflower, thinking they are Jack's beanstalk.

How to grow

Unsurprisingly, sunflowers need to grow in full sun to reach maximum size. Choose a well-drained location, and prepare your soil by digging an area 60–90cm (2–3ft) in circumference to a depth of about 60cm (2ft). Replenish the nutrient supply each season, because sunflowers are hungry plants. Dig in a slow-release granular fertilizer, composted manure and maybe liquid or powdered seaweed for extra complex carbohydrates (these stimulate microscopic soil fungi and microbes to increase the availability of soil nutrients and defend plants against soil-based diseases).

Sunflowers have long taproots that grow fast and become stunted in pots so sow seed direct into the plot. Sow early, as soon as all danger of frost is past and night temperatures are above 10°C (50°F) both day and night. The ideal spacing in rows for giant sunflowers with large seed heads is 50cm (20in) apart. If you have limited space, sow in a small clump that will eventually be thinned to one plant. When sowing seed, first water your soil, then press each seed 2.5cm (1in) deep into the soil, in clumps of 5–6 seeds 15–20cm (6–8in) apart. Slugs and snails may attack, so you will need to protect plants against them. Keep the soil damp.

Seedlings will appear within 5–10 days of sowing. Thin out the runts so there are three left when plants reach 7cm (3in). When they are 30cm (12in) tall, thin them to two, and when they reach 60cm (24in), select the best. Feed often and water regularly. Pour several litres of properly diluted fertilizer around each sunflower every week once the plant reaches 1m (3ft) or so high.

Cut the stalks at the bases when the ripened seeds develop hard shells. If you plan to preserve them for your bird feeder, wait until the seeds are completely dry; then remove them by hand or by rubbing them over wire mesh into a basket.

April

'I used to visit and revisit it a
dozen times a day, and stand
in deep contemplation over my
vegetable progeny with a love that
nobody could share or conceive
of who had never taken part in
the process of creation.'

Nathaniel Hawthorne, *Mosses from an Old Manse*

Grow something new to eat

Each new season grow something out of your comfort zone. This could lead to a failure, but it might also widen your growing knowledge. The new challenge does not have to be just with veg: for example, monkey-puzzle trees were big in the 1970s and became dinner party talking points. These days, it is the veg you grow for the table that impresses other guests, so try pink potatoes, orange beetroot and purple carrots, or stripy aubergines and cauliflowers in green, orange or purple. All are grown in the same way as conventional veg. Or try heirloom Victorian favourites such as salsify, scorzonera and skirret. One of the biggest myths in gardening is that a crop is 'easy to grow'. If the plant is unusual or has fallen out of fashion, this is usually because it is not easy to cultivate or it tastes horrible.

What to grow

Salsify is an unusual veg to try to grow: it looks a bit like parsnip but tastes of oysters, asparagus and, some say, coconut. Stones are the enemy of tapered roots, so sieve them out before sowing into previously manured soil where the leaves will receive full sun. Sow seed 2cm (¾in) deep and the same distance apart two weeks before the last expected frost in spring, then thin seedlings to 5–8cm (2–3in) apart. Keep the soil moist, and harvest four or five months later.

Another unusual crop to try is Chinese cabbage, which grows like lettuce. Use in a salad or lightly cooked with butter.

A good place to look for new challenges, if you want to try something outside your comfort zone, is heirloom varieties, such as the artichoke 'Green Globe'. After harvesting the flower buds, soak them for two hours, then boil until tender; serve with butter. Cardoon 'Rouge d'Alger' is similar to artichoke. Or why not grow heirloom seed of New Zealand spinach?

Exotic fruit is a good bet if you want to grow something that you might just be able to produce cheaper than you can buy. Even fruit bushes such as goji berry and blueberry are comparatively easy. Just buy a young plant and establish it in a sunny place (or in a pot filled with ericaceous compost for blueberries or John Innes No. 2 for goji berries). Blueberries do better in acidic soil and in small groups. Space plants 2m (6ft) apart and feed with tomato fertilizer. You will have to wait two or three years for the fruit, which ripens in late summer.

A fig tree is ideal in a tub or pot. Plant in John Innes No. 3 compost with crocks in the bottom of the pot for drainage. Figs survive well outside, even in winter. Train against walls or fences or just plant in a sunny spot. Apply a foliar feed of seaweed every two weeks or so, and give tomato fertilizer when in fruit.

Brightly coloured crops are a feast for the eyes.

THREE IDEAS: TICKLE YOUR TASTE BUDS

1 **Try growing peppers and chillis indoors**: they will be cheaper than the vegetables you can buy.

2 **Asparagus** takes three years to mature and needs its own bed (in return for a brief cropping season), but it is easy to grow. Just plant a crown and leave it to establish.

3 **Jerusalem artichokes** are perennials so do not need replanting each season. They require a couple of years to mature but, again, are worth the wait because they are easy to cultivate and produce good results.

April

Time to sow . . .

UNDER CLOCHES
- celery • courgettes • dwarf French beans • leeks • pumpkins • sweetcorn • tomatoes

DIRECT IN THE PLOT
- salads

'Deep in the sun-search'd
growths the dragon-fly/
Hangs like a blue thread
loosen'd from the sky...'

Dante Gabriel Rossetti, *Silent Noon*

Time to plant . . .

- asparagus crowns • beetroot
- broad beans • cabbage
- container-grown fruit trees
- fennel • kohl rabi • peas
- potatoes • salsify • scorzonera
- spinach • turnips
- winter brassicas

Time to harvest . . .

- chards • early salad crops
from the greenhouse
- late sprouting broccoli

Get qualified and learn Latin

Study for a Royal Horticultural Society certificate. You will enjoy working on the plot so much more if you know what you are doing and why, rather than just doing the easy stuff or planting by rote as it says in the book. Soil structure, photosynthesis and soil pH may seem like a science lesson, but in gardening you will benefit from understanding them. When you get hold of the course notes, however, you may be surprised at what you already know and so the course may not be too time-consuming.

Carl Linnaeus introduced a simplified system for naming plants some 250 years ago. Battling your way through his structure of family, genus, species, subspecies, variety, form and gender would be hard enough if it were in English, but it is in Latin and that is even more difficult to spell.

How to do it

Common names often tell us nothing about the plant – its origin, shape, form or size – and that is where Latin comes in: for example, *columnaris* means 'shooting up'. Such words help when selecting plants, and they make plants a bit more interesting. A lot of Latin makes sense in English. It is handy to know that *alba* means white, *annua* is annual, *baccata* equals berry-bearing, *floribunda* is free-flowering, *japonica* means Japanese, *niger* is black, *rubens* is red, *virens* is green and *vulgaris* means common.

The main concern is remembering each botanical name, which generally comprises a genus and a species, and sometimes a cultivar or other minor variant. All have to be spelt right.

Also on your RHS course, you will learn about the nitrogen, phosphorus and potassium proportions in farmyard manure, as well as several, different ways to take leaf cuttings, the components of John Innes composts, and that rockwool is made not from sheep's wool, but of fibres spun from molten basalt. You may never use the propagation technique of bulb scaling, but it is handy to know it just in case.

> ### THREE IDEAS: MORE ENLIGHTENMENT
>
> ❶ **Take courses**, gaining practical certificates in chainsaw use, drystone walling, garden machinery maintenance, brushcutting, quad biking, forklift truck driving or tractor driving, for example.
>
> ❷ **Give talks/lectures** for the allotment or horticulture society or record yourself for broadcast on YouTube. You could potentially charge for your talks. See www.gardenmediaguild.co.uk/services/speakers.html for an idea of what to speak about and fees.
>
> ❸ **Retrain for a new career:** sign on for a college-based course in garden design, arboriculture, commercial horticulture or garden centre management.

Understanding Linnaeus's plant-naming system will deepen your interest in gardening.

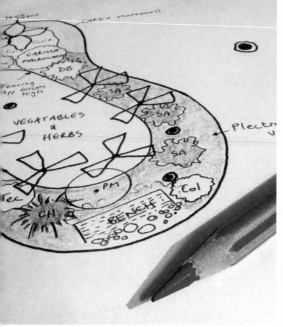

1. Make sure your designs work on paper before committing them to the ground.

2. Calculate plant spacings so you buy enough bedding plants to fill the des

TRANSFORM YOUR PLOT: STEP BY STEP

3. Half an hour before planting, water the plants and let the water soak through.

4. A few weeks after planting and the bedding fills out, covering bare groun

Transform your plot

Every year at flower shows, a few – not many – of the show garden designs are 'literal'. Designers interpret a brief to make plants form objects: for example, a bowl of custard made of yellow blooms or an Olympic oarsman made of topiary and bedding. The traditional kitsch bedding plant display was deemed to lack style because of its literal depictions of town names or coronation crowns, but now these types of designs are increasingly appreciated in an ironic or knowing way.

The RHS Chelsea Flower Show may be the catwalk of garden design, but why not make your plot go beyond fashionable? And if you know what is cool (prairie-style meadows, cloud-pruned trees, modernist geometric paving, subtle tones in your planting, waves of planting, lovely sculpture, expensive garden buildings and rectangular ponds), you can create the opposite as the ultimate anti-fashion statement.

How to do it

Introduce pampas grass, rockeries, animal topiary, words made of bedding, or any plants trained to look like something other than plants.

As well as the council park idea of writing words in plants, usually to commemorate events, you could make a picture from your plants. Garden designers rarely use bedding or veg in the Chelsea show gardens, so use them yourself. The plantless garden, such as the 2009 Chelsea show's 'Paradise in Plasticine' garden, is the ultimate anti-gardening statement and is brilliantly kitsch. Artier still are avant-garde examples such as the biennial Chaumont-sur-Loire Garden Festival or the conceptual garden section of the RHS Hampton Court Flower Show.

I like the idea of a 1970s' dinner-themed design – prawn cocktail, steak 'n' chips with peas, onion rings and mushrooms, and Black Forest gateau. The seaside garden with rope, shells, boat, sand and stones is a classic theme. Instead, think of your plot as the prawn cocktail of gardening, with naff bedding, pampas grass and red hot pokers. How about a Stonehenge on your plot?

To get the right look, set aside a special area. It is pretty daring to use your whole plot. There is no set way to do this, but you do need to use your imagination. Think about plant colours and textures and what will bloom at the same time. Change the scheme seasonally. Bring the outside indoors and create an indoor naff garden with aspidistras, primrose baskets, dyed plants, gaudy cacti, cheese plants, rubber plants, yucca and hyacinths. Why not mix in edibles such as chillis, peppers and herbs?

April

....
....
....
....
....
....
....
....
....
....
....
....
....
....
....

.... 'Show me your garden and
.... I shall tell you what you are.'
.... Alfred Austin, *The Garden that I Love*

THREE IDEAS: CHANGING PLACES

❶ **Create a plantless garden,** using plasticine or Lego. This could be a miniature village or landscape, such as a train running through the countryside.

❷ **Build a rockery,** which was once the most fashionable type of garden, and one that used to dominate the RHS Chelsea Flower Show until the 1950s. Grow alpines in tufa-stone sinks. Recommended rock plants include aubretia, hardy geraniums, ivies, sedums, sempervivum and wild thyme.

❸ **A mannequin** on your plot is good as a scarecrow. Dress it in your old clothes and change these with your mood or season.

Visit gardens and other plots

The National Gardens Scheme is a great source of inspiration. It encourages new ways of looking at gardens when visiting them, and has been prompted by people who like the idea of gardening but do not want to talk about the 'how to'. The idea of gardening rather than the practice appeals to some people who are bored of reading the usual garden staples of hints and tips and fawning reports of visiting gardens. At http://thinkingardens.co.uk, the approach is anything but that practical. Looking around a garden is much more rewarding if you really know what you are looking at; then you will look with a critical eye. It seems a bit harsh to go round other people's allotments taking notes about poor-quality lettuces or weeds between the flagstones, but to critique the style of the plot is a bit more reasonable.

How to do it

Take in a county's (or island's or country's) gardens while on holiday. Read about where you are going first. Park well away from the plot you are visiting so you can put it into context. Keep your senses open – so no sunglasses, headphones or nose masks. Taste and touch plants too (if no one's watching). Do not pick anything. Ask if you can take a cutting.

Talk to the gardener, not the owner, if you really want to know about the garden. Listen into other garden visitors' conversations. Employ a critical eye, as if you were a food or theatre writer. Write a critique of the plot and publish it online on your blog, or try http://thinkingardens. co.uk. Evaluate and assess rather than carp. Also post your pics in the same way food bloggers post photos of their meals. What you like and dislike is as valid as anyone else's thoughts, particularly if you garden yourself.

So many plots and gardens have just evolved. Many gardens are collections of souvenir plants, given as presents and collected as momentoes of foreign holidays – think olives, tree ferns, bottlebrushes and flaxes. Modern allotments are often more designed than your average garden, with regimented rows of raised beds topped off with unweathered larchlap sheds and sturdy new greenhouses. Look for herb knot gardens, finials or obelisks to beckon the eye, fruit cages, pergolas, stumperies, pleached trees, rectangular sunken pools or seating approached by steps. Any visit is great for inspiration. Also, meet old (and make new) gardening friends.

Gardens owned by institutions tend to be more formal, with lots of labels and serried rows of plants, cultivated to strict horticultural standards. The plantsman's garden often has specimens for sale as well as a national collection of one species. Some gardens open to the public throw in a bit of everything that is expensive, such as rills and grand greenhouses.

A trip to the RHS Chelsea Flower Show broadens horticultural horizons.

THREE IDEAS: GREAT DAYS OUT

❶ **Arrange a group garden visit** through the horticultural/allotment society, or with a garden bloggers' or writers' group. Compare notes. Try overseas – *jardins familiaux* or *hortillonnages* in France, or German *kleingarten*.

❷ **Take notes and photos** to remember key moments of inspiration. Maybe publish them. Visit plots that are not just fruit and veg to find a broader perspective.

❸ **Open your own plot** for charity (see www.ngs.org. uk) or open as an individual and advertise locally.

May

"'It always amazes me to look at the little, wrinkled brown seeds and think of the rainbows in 'em," said Captain Jim. "When I ponder on them seeds I don't find it nowise hard to believe that we've got souls that'll live in other worlds. You couldn't hardly believe there was life in them tiny things, some no bigger than grains of dust, let alone colour and scent, if you hadn't seen the miracle, could you?'"

L.M. Montgomery, *Anne's House of Dreams*

Create a private retreat

Gardens are essentially private spaces. And 'public' allotments are, too. Community gardening has its place, but it is rarely on an allotment.

Although a wall of pallets, acting like a palisade around your plot, means 'keep out', it also provides some shelter from wind as well as structure. However, any boundary creates shade, so be wary of overshadowing your plot for the sake of privacy. And beware of hiding away from the plot community, which might start whispering about you.

We all love boundaries in our gardens. Who can imagine gardens without a privet hedge, larchlap fence or brick wall? Today, for many people their allotment is their garden. And still we crave boundaries.

What to do

Place a carpet runner along the edge of your plot to keep down weeds and provide a path. Such a barrier also shows the boundary, and nettles will then have to leap the barrier before getting stuck into your plot.

If your plot divider is not a plant, you might want to grow something up it. Climbers such as rose, honeysuckle and wisteria provide good decoration for a wall or fence. A clock or bird box would also make the fence more interesting, as would a mural.

Once the plot is private, why not take up an instrument that you would not be allowed to play in the house – trumpet, drums and so on. Or you could sunbathe in your private space.

Some bamboo species can be planted to make quick-growing, dense windbreaks or shelter belts that also screen unsightly views. If you are worried about its rampant spread, grow your bamboo plants in pots or establish them as a barrier in a 60cm-(24in-) deep trench and line the sides with slabs, thick root-barrier fabric or corrugated iron, so that the defences protrude above the soil. Plant the bamboo rhizomes, cover with soil, water and mulch.

For edible windbreaks, Jerusalem artichokes work well, as do fruiting hedges. For Jerusalem artichokes, plant tubers in spring 40cm (16in) apart in manured ground. You can stake young stems and cut them down in autumn. Dig up the crop when required.

THREE IDEAS: PUSHING BOUNDARIES

❶ **Mirrors,** even distorting ones, make good barriers, suggesting your plot is bigger than it is.

❷ **Think topsy-turvy:** dig down to create a sunken garden (sides suitably reinforced, of course) or create a boundary in the sky with a tower garden.

❸ **A tree in each corner** with a treehouse on top (or four watchtowers, each with a green roof and climbers up the sides) provides tangible evidence that the plot is yours and you do not want any intruders.

A fence that provides privacy is an important addition for many plot-holders.

May

Time to sow . . .

INDOORS
- cardoons • cucumbers

DIRECT IN THE PLOT
- chards • French beans • runner beans • sweetcorn

Time to harvest . . .

- asparagus • kale • radish
- salad leaves • spring cabbage
- sprouting broccoli
- winter cauliflowers

Time to plant . . .

- courgettes • globe artichokes
- leeks • tomato plugs

Time to transplant . . .

- winter brassicas

....

....

....

....

....

....

....

....

....

....

....

....

....

....

....

'My neighbour asked if he could use my lawnmower and I told him of course he could, so long as he didn't take it out of my garden.'

Eric Morecambe, quoted in *You'll Miss Me When I'm Gone: The life and work of Eric Morecambe* by Gary Morecambe

Party on your plot

Gardening gets popular this month, so make time for an allotment party. The RHS Chelsea Flower Show is on TV and, a bit like after the London Marathon or Wimbledon, middle-class Britain feels a surge of interest in pursuits such as jogging, tennis and gardening. For your plot party, you could have a barbecue, but you do have to include some of your own produce. This is a chance to show off – think Hugh Fearnley-Whittingstall or Jamie Oliver when compiling your menu.

How to get your friends involved

Get some chairs from somewhere, and a table. You will also need plates, cups and cutlery, as well as drink. Music is important, whether recorded or live. LED lighting is becoming more popular for outdoor events. Citronella candles may ward off flying insect pests, and their light may be useful. Bring extra blankets or jumpers in case it gets cold. Ask all your guests to bring something they have grown or made. You will also need a fallback of food such as crisps.

One theme you can use for a party is to harvest a specific crop. So you could host a potato, strawberry or plum party. Kids love this. And the plot-holder gets a free working party.

Another way to theme your event is to make it posh, as an antithesis to the dirty boots worn on the plot. So hold a black-tie party. In case of bad weather, stick up a gazebo or marquee if you are feeling ambitious. A barbecue is the traditional outdoor-eating solution, but you could try a hangi, fish-smoker, bonfire or chimenea. Meat-eaters will love the rusticity of a hog roast, as an alternative to the barbecue. All provide a focus to your event, as well as heat and atmosphere. Patio heaters, while being environmentally suspect, do keep you warm, and they provide light.

Plan your event around the allotment show as an after-party and you are guaranteed plenty of guests – and produce to eat. If you share a plot, then every day is an allotment party, after the obligatory arguments about who hasn't done what.

THREE IDEAS: SOCIAL CIRCLES

❶ **Bushcraft**: sit around whittling sticks and telling tall tales of how big the veg was you once grew.

❷ If drinking friends are not making it to the pub any more because cash is tight, have a **'men around a fire' evening**. Offer a few drinks while you burn non-compostable waste.

❸ **Hold a gig in your garden**: allotments are ideal for setting up stages over a raised bed for mini-Woodstocks. They're away from houses so the noise should not matter. You can also have an audience for your allotment instrument practice.

Let's celebrate – a plot party is the perfect occasion to entertain your friends.

Watch how the experts grow

Modern allotment inspiration on TV began with a cook, rather than a gardener. Jamie Oliver's *Jamie at Home*, twelve-episode series of 2007, featuring lugubrious gardener Brian Skilton, kicked off the grower–cook revolution by saying that good food starts with good ingredients. In each episode, Jamie Oliver made one ingredient the 'hero' of the show, with episodes on: tomatoes; courgettes; barbecue ingredients; beans; onions; carrots and beets; potatoes; peppers and chillies; mushrooms; feathered game; pumpkin and squash; and winter salad.

The series proved how much easier it is to show how to cook a vegetable on TV than how to grow it, simply because you can often cook in real time (or do the 'here is one I made earlier' trick), but it takes ages to grow a vegetable.

What to watch

Nevertheless, gardeners have taken part in dedicated grow-your-own TV. In collaboration with the RHS, Carol Klein wrote and presented the six-part BBC series *Grow Your Own Veg* in the same year as Jamie Oliver's garden–cooking hybrid show. She featured forty food plants with detailed planting advice, and followed that up with *Grow Your Own Fruit*, using a similar format.

Joe Swift included his own allotment on BBC *Gardeners' World* in 2008. He showed how to transform a new plot into a productive one, by making raised beds, erecting a shed and, obviously, growing produce.

Also in 2007, a cinema film called *Grow Your Own* was released. (The film had previously been known under the title *The Allotment*.) In it, a group of refugees were given plots in a Merseyside allotment, but a telecoms company threatened to evict them.

In 2004, Every Picture Media (www.everypicturemedia.co.uk) made the fifteen-part series *The Allotment*, a low-budget production for ITV West. Allotment holder David Cemlyn and head gardener Jane Moore provided a step-by-step guide through the growing calendar while meeting plot-holders who talked about their allotment successes.

Meanwhile, Splash Productions produced the Grow Your Own Channel at www.thegrowyourownchannel.tv featuring thirty films on allotment production, and the Horticultural Channel offers more low-budget allotment films.

Useful websites to check for advice and discussion include www.allotment.org.uk, www.soilman.net, www.allotments4all.co.uk and the membership groups www.jardins-familiaux.org (France), www.kleingarten-bund.de (Germany), www.nagstrust.org, www.sags.org.uk and www.nsalg.org.uk (UK).

Finally, James Wong's 2009 ethnobotany BBC series *Grow Your Own Drugs* is available on DVD.

What's on? Television gardening will inspire and inform.

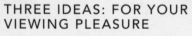

THREE IDEAS: FOR YOUR VIEWING PLEASURE

❶ **For light relief**, watch the ITV horticultural crime series *Rosemary and Thyme* featuring Felicity Kendal of the 1970s' grow-your-own comedy series *The Good Life* (both *Rosemary and Thyme* and *The Good Life* are available on DVD).

❷ **Film your own** grow-your-own lesson on a camcorder and put it on YouTube, and rack up the hits.

❸ **Write to a TV company** with your idea for a gardening show.

1. Habitats are needed for all kinds of wildlife, from a drilled log to hollow sticks.

2. A compost heap is good for wildlife, both a habitat and a place to find foo

CREATE A WILDLIFE AREA: STEP BY STEP

3. Introducing a small pond will significantly increase the range of visitors to your plot.

4. A north-east-facing bird box is an ide way to attract and accommodate bird

Create a wildlife area

Far from being a nuisance, wildlife such as hedgehogs, birds, bats, frogs and toads will help to keep garden pests under control. For too long, gardeners have been at war with such creatures. Saying you like wildlife gardening is often a front for actually using any means necessary to keep animals off your plot. Time for a change. Allow nettles to grow, leave piles of old wood and stones around and let your compost heap overspill. All will attract the wild animals that will make your plot life so much richer.

Nettles are great host plants for caterpillars of the small tortoiseshell and peacock butterflies. They're also invaluable as a cooked, spinach-like vegetable or for a liquid fertilizer when rotted in a bucket of water. Relocate nettles dug up from waste ground and water them in. They like disturbed ground. A nettle patch will grow without much encouragement, and will hold overwintering aphids, which provide an early food source for ladybirds. These same aphids are eaten in large numbers by blue tits and other woodland birds. In late summer nettle seed provides a food source for seed-eating birds. But keep a well-trodden path around your nettle patch or they will spread out of control.

What to do

Of course, there is more to bringing in wildlife than encouraging nettles. A wood pile (the older the wood the better) makes a good nest for hibernating hedgehogs, as well as many minibeasts such as woodlice. Slug-eating slow worms might shelter there. Buried wood feeds the soil (the permaculture technique of *hugelkultur*) and encourages soil life. Looking above ground, hedgehogs might also nest in your compost heap, if you leave them alone – so might mice. Insects and worms will live in it, and they will attract birds. Hedges, particularly those bearing berries such as holly, berberis and hawthorn, will attract birds and provide a habitat for hedgehogs, voles and shrews. Wild flowers such as bird's foot trefoil, vetch, hawkweed, wild white clover and bluebell will attracts birds and insects, as will plants such as buddleia, scabious, Michaelmas daisy, phlox, sweet William, marigold, sunflower, ornamental grasses, pyracantha, broom, snowberry and cotoneaster.

Amphibians enjoy hiding under rockery stones. They also need water. Diving beetles, water scorpions and mammals looking for a drink will love a pond too. A bog garden, which is safer for young children to be around, will attract the same creatures. Line a shallow depression with pond liner. Fill two-thirds with soil, then top up with water. Plant meadowsweet, loosestrife, marsh marigold, ragged robin, cuckoo flower, cotton grass, bog pimpernel, and creeping Jenny.

Hedgehog, bird and bat boxes might encourage wildlife to your plot. Secure bird boxes in trees and high on fences, well away from where cats can get at them. Place hedgehog boxes on the ground in an overgrown spot.

'The most humiliating thing to me about a garden is the lesson it teaches of the inferiority of man. Nature is prompt, decided, inexhaustible.'

Charles Dudley Warner, *My Summer in a Garden*

....

....

....

....

....

....

....

....

....

....

....

....

....

....

....

....

....

....

....

....

....

....

....

....

....

....

....

....

....

THREE IDEAS: CREATURE COMFORTS

❶ Minibeast zoo or hotel: pile natural materials such as wood, stone, hollow stems and canes into a tower and place on ground where beasts looking for refuge can crawl in.

❷ Butterfly houses: use wire netting to make a hanging cage and put out sugar water for sustenance. Place pupae (bought online at www.wwb.co.uk) in the cage. When they pupate into butterflies, set them free to find a mate.

❸ Fox pillboxes: birdwatchers and observers of foxes might like to build a peephole hide from which to view birds and foxes.

Share the burden

Plot-sharing is a good idea if you decide your allotment is taking up too much time or if you start off with the idea of communal growing being a better plan than having sole responsibility. A group of people looking after one plot takes the pressure off waiting lists and lightens the burden of one-person maintenance. If the waiting list is too long, club together to buy part of a field to share, or suggest a group plot to your employer if they have spare land that might be suitable.

One advantage of group enterprise is the positive nature of such an endeavour. Growing together feels great and achieves something that would be incredibly hard work when done by a single person. It also builds bonds between people and strengthens relationships. Of course, this working/leisure relationship could potentially do the opposite if some people are not seen to be pulling their weight.

Further advantages of a communal plot include sharing the costs, including that of expensive equipment such as mowers, and spreading the watering and weeding load during the growing season.

However, sharing a plot can be harder for some than others to take part in. Some may live close to the plot, while others may live farther away on the other side of town and will not be able to visit so often.

Some members of the shared plot may not appreciate just how much weeding is needed at certain times of year, and a lot of extra graft may be required if you also have invasive species that require repeated and laborious efforts to keep them in check or clear them.

How to do it

Come up with a plan each year with beds allocated between everyone to look after. Meet up regularly to discuss what the main jobs are and share them out. Some people are better at organizing, seed sowing and potting on, while others are more suited to digging, shed or greenhouse repairs and DIY jobs. Pool your resources and compete to provide crops from the allotment. Keep a communications book in the shed so that everyone knows what is going on. Hand in receipts each year and share the cost equally.

The shared allotment is a great way to socialize on summer evenings and weekends, but barbecues will lead to more socialising than work. If you are good friends, you may already have a clear understanding of how much work each of you is prepared to do so you may not be disappointed by each other's level of commitment.

Community chest – a plot shared can be a problem halved.

THREE IDEAS: HELPING HANDS

❶ www.landshare.net had more than 70,000 members in 2013. TV cook Hugh Fearnley-Whittingstall set up the plot-sharing scheme in 2009. Now, with so many members, the aim is to connect those who have land to share with those who need land for cultivating food.

❷ Sublet a bit of your plot to the unemployed, if rules allow; in return for their labour allow them to take half the produce.

❸ Be a plot-share mentor, helping others to grow their own. Be a kids' mentor by setting up a children's club at the plot as a form of babysitting so the adults can get on with gardening. Also, teach the youngsters about the joys of growing your own.

June

'One of the most tragic things I know about human nature is that all of us tend to put off living. We are all dreaming of some magical rose garden over the horizon instead of enjoying the roses that are blooming outside our windows today.'

Dale Carnegie, *How to Win Friends and Influence People*

THREE IDEAS: NEIGHBOURHOOD WATCH

❶ **Sheds**: padlock doors and lock (or board up) windows, mark and lock expensive tools (or remove them), repair holes in the walls, set an alarm or use a communal, metal, alarmed container for the storage of valuable items from all the allotments on your site.

❷ **Allotment shops**: mark stock, hold regular stock takes, do not leave cash overnight and display a sign saying so. Fix weak points in the shop structure. Better still, engage young people in the site so they have a sense of ownership and value the facilities.

❸ **Big signs displaying allotment rules,** opening hours, contact details of the allotment owner and how to report crimes act as deterrents too.

Crack down on crime

Allotment crime is on the up. However, what may seem to be damage by dastardly thieves is quite possibly caused by birds. So get some netting or a fruit cage to deter them.

While you might think burglars are to blame for most plot crime, the most likely cause of dispute on the allotment is neighbourhood arguments. Splitting plots to give more people a chance to own one has brought people into closer proximity and creates a greater risk of rows. This can be over boundaries, weeds, who has the biggest veg or about an eviction notice, and it can escalate so weedkiller can end up on your prized veg or lawn, or tools can 'go missing'.

Of course, the real allotment crime is by developers and councils who want to sell off plots. This is thankfully rare now, such is the demand for plots and publicity around them.

While falling out with your neighbours is a matter for personal reconciliation, straightforward theft can be deterred by simple locks on your shed door and allotment gates, alongside strong fences around the plot perimeter. Most at risk of theft are tools. Burning down sheds has been an issue that has led to bans on plot building in some areas.

What to do

Patrolling or camping at night may put off thieves. Night-vision goggles or infrared cameras might help. But be aware of the data protection laws if you use CCTV or other filming techniques. Make sure the CCTV is monitored and recordable, with signs saying it is there as a deterrent.

Some police are using a forensic liquid, with a unique DNA-style code that can be painted on to any items of value such as garden tools and lawnmowers. If marked property is stolen and later recovered by police, the forensic coding, which shows up only under ultraviolet light, can be used to identify the true owner and link a suspect with a crime scene.

Plot fencing should be in good condition, and preferably be in the form of open railed/welded mesh, 2m (6ft) high with no gaps. Consider planting thorny shrubs inside the fence at low level to deter climbing. Such plants also contribute to biodiversity. Cut down trees that can be used to climb over fences, and remove compost bins that might be used to get over a fence or wall.

Gates should be locked and have anti-climb features. They should deter people who want to drive in and fly tip; lockable or electronic, collapsible bollards could help there, too.

Light your allotment at night, especially if paths run by it. If you alarm your shed, be ready to turn it off if the siren goes off at the wrong time. Consider GPS alarms, which tag machinery so it can be tracked.

Lock up shop. Vigilance is the key to allotment security.

Building raised beds

Many new allotments include raised beds because they provide the ideal growing conditions for many vegetables. Raised beds allow you to control more easily the soil's moisture, fertility and weediness. On the other hand, these high-sided grow-boxes take up more space than food plants that are growing in the open ground, and unwelcome slugs seem to like the corners under the wooden sides of the beds. But, filled with soil, they provide the excellent drainage needed to grow both vegetables and flowers really well.

The soil in raised beds avoids becoming compacted because you do not stand or walk on it. These beds also help you to get organized because they are more regimented than open-ground growing, and they warm up more quickly in spring. You can grow plants closer together too.

The ready-made, slot-in kits for raised beds that you can buy sidestep the need for a carpentry degree. Nevertheless, you might prefer to make your own raised bed, so here is what you need to know to make one.

Get the look

You will need: pressure-treated softwood planks, 38 x 225mm (1½ x 8⅘in), such as larch wood; stakes, 300 x 25mm (12 x 1in); and 75mm (3in) galvanized screws or nails.

Keeping things simple, the basic raised bed should not test your joinery skills too much. Orient the bed north to south for maximum sun exposure. Clear the site of weeds and level it.

Mark out the bed with stakes and string, and check the levels. To support the sides, drive in the stakes one at each corner of the raised bed and one stake for every 1–1.5m (3–5ft) along the side of the bed; drive them in so they are 60 per cent buried in the ground. You can check they are straight vertically and horizontally with a spirit level. Nail or screw the first planks to the retaining stakes so they are partly buried. Fix the next row of boards to the stakes on top of the base layer.

Break up the soil surface to improve drainage. Add hardcore if the bed is deep. Enrich the soil with manure and new topsoil. You can paint or stain the planks, and seal gaps with waterproof self-adhesive tape on the inside.

A timber-post raised bed needs a 40cm (16in) trench half-filled with gravel for the timber post 'fence'. Butt your posts together in the trench, making sure they are all standing at the same height. Pour in a 20cm (8in) layer of concrete to fix the posts and line the sides of the bed with a waterproof membrane.

Raised beds that are built with walls of brick or railway sleepers are other options, but more complex to build.

ace a raised bed on sunny, open ground
ing a ready-made kit or make your own.

2. Clear the site and level it before marking
out and driving in stakes at the corners.

BUILD A RAISED BED: STEP BY STEP

ll with fresh, fertile soil and level gently.
t the soil settle before planting.

4. Raised beds provide a well-organized
space for growing lots of crops up close.

Time to sow . . .

DIRECT IN THE PLOT
- Chinese cabbage • peas
- radicchio • salads • turnips

'Do not spread the compost on the weeds.'

Shakespeare, *Hamlet*

Time to harvest . . .

- beetroot • chards • early carrots
- early potatoes • forced rhubarb
- greenhouse salads • herbs
- Japanese onions • peas • radish
- spinach • summer cabbage
- young turnips

Time to plant . . .

- celeriac • celery • courgettes
- cucumbers • pumpkins
- runner beans • sweetcorn
- tomatoes • winter brassicas

THREE IDEAS: RAISED EXPECTATIONS

1 Build a raised bed on legs: this avoids back pain, weed-seed spread and, depending on the height, stops some animals climbing in and nibbling your seedlings. It is good for wheelchair gardeners, too – unlike roof gardens, which do have the benefits of using all your space and dodging the worst of the weeds and pests. A skip is the ultimate raised bed.

2 Protect your raised bed: mount rigid PVC pipes inside its wooden frame, then slot flexible hoops on to them, to hold bird netting over your crops.

3 As an alternative to a wooden bed, use **concrete paving slabs** raised on end and half buried for the walls. You will need to fill the bottom of the bed with hardcore for drainage.

THREE IDEAS: FUN & GAMES

❶ Send them on safari: get them to hunt bugs, with magnifying glasses and identification cards. Bribe them with a penny a weed to clear your plot.

❷ Start a sunflower-growing race.

❸ Make potato prints: cut a tuber in half and cut out a design (adult help will be needed here). Dip the end in poster paint and print on a card.

Keep children occupied

Small children do not like helping in the garden. Adults often do not like them there either. Gardens can be cold, wet, dirty and dangerous. However, kids can be cheap labour and benefit from being useful instead of spending life feeling merely ornamental. Payment is a good incentive for most of us to work. Do not even think of 'interesting them in gardening' – can you think of anything more boring and off-putting for a healthy youngster? Wait until he or she is old, like you. Nevertheless, as children get older, aged three onwards, they can copy what you do on the plot, by growing a few potatoes or lettuces or sunflowers. This gives them some ownership, but you can go further and make the plot a child's paradise. What do children like doing? Playing games – not Xbox, but healthy, outdoor fun. Think of your own childhood's outdoor highlights.

Get started

Here are some ideas beyond children helping with what you do on your plot, in miniature. Make a scarecrow: use an old mannequin or nail a crosspiece of wood high up on a post, for arms. An old football can do for a head if you cut a hole in it to stick on the post. Tights, sacks and pillowcases, stuffed with straw or material make the body. Tie them on to the post. Dress the scarecrow in old clothes. Draw on a face. Remember boots and a hat. A CD bird scarer is a variation on this theme.

Treasure hunts work well – hidden toys, Easter eggs, buried treasure. Kids like being pirates. And they like toys and chocolate.

The obvious solution of buying a slide or climbing frame works well. A tabletop pond and a sandpit are good additions. The pond can be an old washing-up bowl filled with real pond water and weeds. Just see what beasts develop. The technique for a sandpit is to dig a hole in the ground. It is much easier than making a wooden sandbox. Line with landscaping fabric and pin the sides with stakes, hammered in flush. Use it for children's beach volleyball or long jump.

Children will play with whatever is around. The shed can be a den; the wheelbarrow is a vehicle; the compost heap is for climbing; while the water trough is just dangerous: supervised hosing of children is much safer and more fun.

And if you must get them growing, try it in a pot they have painted (recycled cups or tins appeal to their little minds). The old favourite cress head is a good start. Place some wet kitchen towel in the bottom of a yogurt pot and put some damp cotton wool on top of that with cress seeds spread and squashed on top. Place it in the shed window and watch it grow.

Kids' stuff – memories are made on the plot.

June

'…there need nobody run short o' victuals if the land was made the most on, and there was never a morsel but what could find its way to a mouth.'

George Eliot, *Silas Marner*

Camp on your plot

The beach hut or second home is a dream for many urban dwellers. It is a sign you have made it, and it is a cheap holiday. Some ways to have a home away from home are to camp or have a caravan or camper van. While it may not be practical or economical to have a vehicle to camp in, you have a ready-made site to go on 'holiday' to if you have an allotment or back garden. The difference is that the allotment camping experience is an urban one, and as such offers a heightened experience in comparison to a campsite. A tent is required, unless your shed or greenhouse is suitable.

Camping on your plot is common in Denmark, where allotment gardens are a popular breathing space for town and city dwellers. Small cabins – often not much bigger than a shed – gorgeous flower beds, red chequered tablecloths, chats across the garden fence and the Danish flag flying on a Sunday are the idyllic image many Danes have of life in an allotment garden. Danish allotments are often on the outskirts of towns and cities. Waiting lists are long, but plots are big, at around 400sq. m (478sq. yd), so they are worth waiting for. Owners are allowed to live in their cabins throughout the summer when the association's mains-water tap is on – a bit like some British beach huts. There is no water in the area during winter, and it has no sewage system – the toilets being emptied via a gully. Some owners have installed their own solar panels on the roof, while the rest of the association's members do without electricity.

Allotments are popular in the Czech Republic, the Netherlands, Germany, Scandinavia and Russia, among other countries. Indeed, continental-European allotments, of which 3 million are represented by the Office International du Coin de Terre et des Jardins Familiaux, have broader uses for such plots than in the UK. As well as community and environmental functions, allotments have socio-cultural and economic roles. Enshrined in the Danish way of life are ideas about meaningful leisure spaces for families; relaxation spaces for after work; places for the unemployed to grow cheap food and to feel useful and to help immigrants integrate within the host society; facilities for the disabled to participate in social life and for senior citizens to find self-fulfilment during retirement.

What to do

You probably are not allowed to camp in UK allotments, so be discreet, arrive late and leave early (after clearing up all evidence). Camping on your plot is life enhancing: it is as straightforward as putting up your tent. For a toilet, you might need a bucket; but wash in the water tank and maybe have a barbecue. Bring a torch, enjoy the silence or turn on the radio. You will probably hear nocturnal animals, and are likely to see foxes.

You can retreat to a tent in the garden on a warm, sleepy afternoon.

THREE IDEAS: UNDER CANVAS

❶ **Glamping** (which is glamorous camping): get someone to bring you breakfast in a yurt, tepee or safari tent.

❷ **Take a telescope** along with your camping gear down to the plot and see the sky at night.

❸ **Garden at night** by the rhythm of the moon (see page 170).

July

'The glory of gardening:
hands in the dirt, head in
the sun, heart with nature.
To nurture a garden is to
feed not just the body,
but the soul.'

Alfred Austin, *The Garden that I Love*

Dinner on your plot

Entertain on your plot for a novel dining experience. Serve home-grown produce for the full effect. You could include your chickens and eggs as well as fruit, veg and herbs. Maybe handcrafted preserves too.

After a zen-like day with your fingers in the dirt, get scrubbed up and make dinner on your plot. A camping gas stove gives more options (such as cooking up a big paella), unless you have a deluxe barbecue, on which you can cook pizza, bread and just about anything else you like. A buffet of finger foods is easiest.

Allotment dining is about taking the indoor experience of eating outside, in the same way that you might eat *al fresco*, but extending the experience to your plot.

Maybe hold a 'Come dine with me' competition with fellow plot-holders over a weekend, or over four or five weeks, where you compete to cook the best meal among your peers. Give scores out of ten and organize a prize. Stipulate home-grown or home-produced food.

If you have a paddling pool, pretend it is a hot tub for the classic 'Come dine with me' moment at the end of a drunken meal.

What to do

Ideally, the event needs to be in summer. Use anti-mosquito candles and patio heaters. Make sure you use placemats, napkins, cut glass and fine china, and hire a butler, for the full dinner party effect. Play darts, quoits or giant Jenga as well as eating.

It is more important to consider what food is practical to serve outdoors than what is possible to cook in the kitchen.

When you are cooking or serving outdoors, be careful to avoid cross-contamination of raw and cooked meat and other ready-to-eat foods. Keep cold foods cold and hot foods hot, because bacteria can grow more quickly in warm summer conditions.

Leave chilled food in the coolbag for as long as possible before taking it out. You should also protect food from contamination by insects, birds, animals and people by keeping it covered whenever possible. Think about handwashing facilities, even if it is just a bucket full of fresh water.

> ### THREE IDEAS: DINNER DATES
>
> ❶ **Menu:** make it all home-grown. Get your garden-expert guests to guess which variety of each plant you have cooked.
>
> ❷ **Invite your allotment committee** to dinner on your plot – you will never receive a 'dirty plot' notice after that.
>
> ❸ Have as guests to your plot dinner your **allotment neighbours** and ask them to bring something they have each grown and cooked. If you do not know them well, all the better for building a community.

Food for thought: show off your produce in the ultimate location – your plot.

Avoid the glut

To avoid a glut plant only a little of everything. Plant a 45cm (18in) row of lettuce and not a full packet. Plant early, mid- and late-season potatoes to spread out your harvests.

However, if the weather is right, you will still have too much of something every year to eat before it goes off. Therefore, the crop needs preserving, for example in a chest freezer in the garage. Back in the 1970s' *Good Life* era, there were loads of books on 'deep freezing' (as there were on using microwaves a decade later). There were also plenty of books on preserves and condiments. A generation later, the advice on making jam and chutney is back, this time on TV and on the internet.

What to do

Making jam is the best way to deal with a glut of fruit. Crab apples, blackcurrants, gooseberries, plums, redcurrants, cooking apples, cranberries, damsons, quince, raspberries, loganberries, boysenberries, tayberries, apricots, blackberries, blueberries, strawberries, rhubarb, elderberries, peaches, sweet cherries, dessert apples, pears, figs and marrows are all great ingredients for jams. Use a big, stainless-steel pan.

Every fruit needs slightly different treatment. For blackcurrants, gently heat the fruit (home-frozen is fine) for about an hour in water. Add the same amount of sugar and stir until it dissolves. Boil rapidly for ten minutes for a couple of jars'-worth, or longer if you have more fruit. When the jam reaches 104°C (220°F), it should be at setting point. Test by putting a teaspoonful on to a cold plate. Chill, then push the outer edge of the jam puddle into the centre with your index finger; if the jam wrinkles it will set. Alternatively, just hold the plate upside down and hope the jam does not fall to the floor. If the jam is overboiled, the mixture will become very sticky. Underdone jam is worse, because it is just fruity, sugary water.

When the jam has reached the proper setting point, skim off any scum, then use a jug to pour the jam into sterilized (cleaned in boiling water and thoroughly dried or 'cooked' in the oven for ten minutes) jars and cover each with a lid immediately.

ick 2kg (4lb 6oz) of ripe strawberries; oid damaged ones. Hull and halve.

2. Mash the fruit to a pulp and put in a thick-bottomed, stainless-steel pan to heat.

MAKE STRAWBERRY JAM: STEP BY STEP

tir in 1.7kg (3lb) of jam sugar and the ice of two lemons. Boil for 15 minutes.

4. When the jam sets, pour into sterilized jars. Cover with waxed paper discs; seal.

July

Time to sow . . .

DIRECT IN THE PLOT
- autumn and winter salads
- beetroot • carrots • lettuce
- peas • spring cabbage • turnips

THREE IDEAS: PRESERVING FRESHNESS

❶ Pickle: choose crunchy and raw veg such as onions, cauliflower or beetroot. Quickly boil (for one minute). Use white wine vinegar and pure pickling salt. Put in a jar, then seal and refrigerate. Sauerkraut is an option too. Salt your cabbage and put in an airtight jar. The released brine will ferment over a week, pickling the veg. Also try making piccalilli.

❷ Green tomato chutney (ideal to use up a late-season glut): use 600g (1lb 5oz) tomatoes and 150ml (5fl. oz) malt or white wine vinegar. Add 175g (6oz) brown sugar, one onion, 125g (4oz) sultanas, chilli flakes, peppercorns, coriander seeds, cloves and bay leaves to taste. Simmer chutney to a thick purée for an hour, then pour into a sterilized jar and seal. Store for three months before eating.

❸ Freeze berries and beans: open-freeze berries on a tray, then break them up and put in a plastic bag/box so the fruit does not stick together. Blanche beans in boiling water for two minutes, then plunge in cold water and freeze in bags. Braised red cabbage freezes well. Stone plums and freeze in a sugar syrup (250g/9oz sugar to 570ml/20fl. oz water, heated until the sugar dissolves). Gently cook the plums in the syrup, then cool and freeze. For 450g (1lb) of fruit, you need 250ml (9fl. oz) syrup. Purée strawberries and apples before freezing. Also freeze sliced apple dipped in water with added lemon juice. Dry herbs in warm air. Storing excess root veg under straw on your plot for the winter is another option.

Time to plant . . .

- winter brassicas

Time to harvest . . .

- beans • brassicas • carrots
- garlic • globe artichokes
- herbs • kale • kohl rabi • onions
- peas • potatoes • salads
- shallots • tomatoes • turnips

THREE IDEAS: VINTAGE CHARM

❶ **Collect early seed catalogues** for inspiration about heritage varieties to grow, and also for historical interest.

❷ **Split botanical art books** into prints to frame (frowned on by book lovers) to decorate your house or to sell individually.

❸ **Read your gardening literature classics** in the comfort of your plot shed. Memoirs, plant-hunter tales, books from famous old gardeners and old garden guides provide particular interest. See www.abebooks.co.uk to compare prices of second-hand books. It is what the professionals use. Pre-twentieth-century gardening literature will always appreciate in value, but later works make less certain investments.

Your vintage collection could be valuable as well as useful.

Collect vintage tools and books

Realising the value and collectability of vintage garden tools, books and plants is a good way to deepen interest in your plot.

For a classic, rainy-day way to enjoy gardening without actually gardening, visit second-hand shops for quirky gardening tools or old garden tomes.

Vintage is now a fashionable gardening look you can create in your own plot. The rustic-looking but built-to-last implements and furniture look fabulous displayed (or even used) inside or outside. Then there are garden antiques – stoneware and sculptures that are available from salvage yards and antique shops. These curios make classic talking points as well as being beautiful pieces of craft in their own right.

Vintage is cool, as we all know, with the new nostalgia related to the current tough times, in which people try to hold on to what they feel is safe and comforting. Warm and fuzzy memories from the past or from your childhood generally provide a powerful reminder of good times, a time when you did not have the stresses of adult life.

What to collect

Most sought after are watering cans, children's tools and curios such as cucumber straighteners, grape storage bottles, hot-bed thermometers and seed measures. Small galvanized watering cans are rare and cost 25 per cent more than standard (10 litre/2 gallon) watering cans. A labelled vintage item, such as a Haws can, attracts a premium.

Forks, spades, hand tools, hoes and rakes from the 1950s and earlier are also commonly collected because nostalgic buyers use them as well as valuing their provenance, balance and quality. Dealers confirm that people use 98 per cent of what they buy, and that customers are gardeners first, and collectors second.

Painted café-style tables and chairs, plant stands, garden cloches, terracotta rhubarb forcers, lead planters and garden coppers are all collectable. The most keenly sought furniture is old, folding bandstand chairs. Trugs, carts, garden furniture and stoneware are also desirable, as are cast-iron troughs. Look for authentic French or British products, unless you prefer vintage-style modern copies, which are widely available.

Poking around antique or junk shops, auctions, charity shops and car boot sales to find bargains might just be the thing to inspire you to get back on the allotment again this spring. Also check skips, sheds and attics for hidden gems.

Restoration projects might be fun, too, if you like that sort of thing. Garden & Wood will restore your old tools (www.gardenandwood.co.uk).

July

....
....
....
....
....
....
....
....
....
....
....
....
....
....
....
....
....
....
....
....

'No occupation is so delightful to me as the culture of the earth, and no culture comparable to that of the garden.'

Thomas Jefferson, letter to Charles W. Peale

Create a natural playground

The natural playground is a wonderful addition to any plot or garden. While shiny metal and plastic playgrounds are prevalent at municipal parks, on your plot the natural look might fit in better. You do not need DIY skills to make your plot fun. Children should learn how to play imaginatively, and while doing so may improve their health.

Get the look

A stack of big sticks and branches leaning against a tree makes brilliant shelter material for kids. They can endlessly arrange them into new dens.

A willow tunnel is a fantastic plaything for children. Simply cut lengths of willow and plant them 1m (39in) apart for as long as you want your tunnel to be. Bend and twist them around each other as they meet in the middle. Plant two willow 'whips' as diagonals alongside each vertical to tie in and hold the structure together. They are the perfect hideaway and socializing place for children, and they help them learn about sustainability too. Kids can also experience how a living sculpture evolves. They can get involved by weaving in new growth.

Stepping stones made from stumpy logs are great, and rope swings bring back the memories of childhood for adults. You need a strong, mature tree. Either tie a rope around a branch or buy a swing seat, tyre swing or ladder to attach to it.

A sandpit is great fun, as is a paddling pool. Paddling pools can be good for splashing or as sandboxes, saving you the hassle of digging,

lining and carpentry. They are usually bought as preformed plastic or blow-up pools. You can fill them with water or play sand. You can also buy old play equipment such as slides and trampolines on the internet. Families grow out of them, and they are bulky so are often given away. A shade sail or retractable umbrella is good protection from sun (and rain). You may need a pile driver to get the supports into the ground so it is best to have them installed by specialists. Alternatively, place your play features under a tree to benefit from its shade.

THREE IDEAS: FOR PLAYTIME

❶ **For little ones**, making mud pies or sieving and piling up gravel are simple ideas.

❷ **Artificial turf** is good as a base for a play area, as are bouncy tyre chips, woodchips or sand.

❸ **Build your own skatepark** or BMX track: install a zipwire if you are feeling adventurous.

Add a shelter, swing, sandpit or log steps to spark kids' imaginations.

THREE IDEAS: HUMBLE ABODES

❶ A **treehouse** on your plot is not just great for the kids but also as sanctuary for adults to get 'up on the roof' and have a bird's eye view of the world.

❷ A **kennel** to keep your working hounds, or a pigeon loft for your flock, are quirky structures to build on your plot (if bye-laws allow).

❸ An underground **nuclear shelter** or Anderson shelter could be just the thing for a military history buff.

Invest in a shed

Shelter is a must on your plot: it brings the leisure into gardening and reduces some of the work. Apart from the obvious functions of storage and hiding from the rain, a shed can be a home away from home. Make tea or drink your home-made allotment wine, sit down and talk to your allotment friends or simply avoid life in your sanctuary. A battery-powered radio is a good addition, as is a kettle and comfy chair – maybe a torch if you have no electricity. The ideal size for a shed is around 12sq. m (14sq. yd). Build it off the ground on a concrete slab or bricks so that air can circulate underneath.

A greenhouse can have the double use of shelter and plant-growing space. However, it may get too hot in summer and too cold in winter. The solution is to cover one end of the greenhouse with a blanket or sheet to keep off the sun in summer and to retain the heat in winter. A paraffin heater is an option as well.

What to do

Sheds can be made from wood, corrugated plastic, metal and even an old Anderson shelter. They each need a hardstanding if they are to stand upright. But it is easier, if more expensive, to buy a flat pack and put it up. For some people, even that is challenging, so why not pay for the DIY store to deliver and put it up for you?

Some sheds have to be painted in allotment colours. If they do not, decorating your shed is fun. Stick a clock on it, and perhaps a thermometer, to start building your own weather station. Use guttering to collect rainwater into a barrel. Grow hops, honeysuckle or roses up it on hooks and wires.

For a cool, green shed roof, to attract birds and insects as well as prevent run-off and provide insulation, line the roof of your shed with a piece of plywood wrapped in waterproof butyl lining, or you can use liquid-painted or spray-on waterproofing. This will protect the roof of the shed from any potential water damage. Then add a drainage mat and 2–6cm (¾–2½ in) of growing media (potting compost and perlite is light and gives good drainage), which must be contained by a wooden frame so the plants stay on the roof.

Alternatively, moss is neglected as a possibility for green roofs. Spread moss fragments on your growing media on the roof. Use water-retention gel and water frequently to establish the moss. Sedum matting is also a popular low-maintenance choice and ideal for a weaker roof. A living carpet of sedum plants is grown on special matting and can be placed over the waterproof layer. Sedums can also be grown in small pockets moulded into a tray. There is no need to lay a drainage layer or substrate as this is all included in the module. Herbs work too on green roofs.

August

'Many gardeners will agree
that hand-weeding is not the
terrible drudgery that it is
often made out to be. Some
people find in it a kind of
soothing monotony. It leaves
their minds free....'

Christopher Lloyd, *The Well-Tempered Gardener*

Bring out a barbecue

Just take a barbecue to your allotment. Charcoal is probably easier than gas to carry – and to dispose of afterwards. Gas grills are more expensive and are popular in barbecue-savvy countries such Australia and the USA, where not much charcoal is used. Some colder countries in the northern hemisphere do not barbecue much, although barbecuing is extremely popular in Scandinavia.

Cook something – preferably that you have grown on your plot. It does not have to be surf and turf on the beach for barbecues to work. Communal barbecuing as a social event and fundraiser for all allotment holders is an idea. A spit roast works really well.

Get the look

Bring out your inner bricklayer – building walls is enormously satisfying – and a brick barbecue in the corner of your plot or for all plot-holders to use creates a useful permanent feature. You need a cooking tray, bricks, sand, water, cement, a spirit level, chisel, hammer and a bricklayer's trowel.

For a crude brick barbecue – ten bricks high and shaped like a rectangle with one long side missing, you will need a flat site. Lay out a single level of bricks. Mix five parts sand to one part cement, adding water until stiff. Set the bricks in cement. Use a spirit level to check that the first level is flat and a set square to check the corners are at right angles. Lay more layers, so the bricks overlap the joints of bricks beneath. You will need to halve some bricks to fill in gaps. Check that it is square all the time. Go seven bricks high. Then put in a brick on each side, perpendicular to the layer below, to support the charcoal tray. Lay three more layers, anchoring metal hooks

in the cement between each layer, to act as supports for the grill trays.

Traditional barbecuing is done slowly with low cooking temperatures and a lot of smoke. Grilling depends on a higher temperature to sear what you are cooking to retain the juices. Here are some tips for grilling.

Make sure whatever you are cooking is not too thick, or it will burn on the outside by the time the inside is done. Start with a scrubbed, clean grill. Brush it or spray it with vegetable oil to prevent food from sticking.

Preheat the grill 15–30 minutes before you intend to start cooking. Have all your cooking tools and meat and veg ready. Marinading should be done already, soaking to taste. You can use a thermometer to check if the cooking temperature is correct. For steak, 46–49°C (115–120°F) is rare, 52–55°C (125–130°F) is medium rare and 60–65°C (140–150°F) is medium. Take food hygiene seriously by cooking meat right through.

Grow it, cook it, eat it. There's nothing better than barbecuing on your plot.

THREE IDEAS: COOKING OUTDOORS

❶ Hangi: dig a pit in the ground, heat stones in the pit with a large fire, placing baskets of food on top of the stones, cover the food, then cover everything with soil for several hours before lifting the hangi.

❷ Chimenea: a metal or terracotta garden heater that was originally used in Mexico for cooking, as its design allows more air to be drawn than a fire basket. Burn oak, cherry (good for flavouring fish) or apple (good for pork ribs) wood for its aromatic scent and its bug-repellent qualities. Put a potato to bake in its heat. Or cater on a grand scale and build a fish-smoker.

❸ Firepit: a metal basket like a brazier for warmth or with a grill on top for cooking.

Time to sow . . .
DIRECT IN THE PLOT
• Japanese onions • parsley
• salads • spring cabbage

'A vegetable garden in the beginning looks so promising and then after all little by little it grows nothing but vegetables, nothing, nothing but vegetables.'

Gertrude Stein, *Wars I Have Seen*

Time to plant . . .

• strawberries

Time to harvest . . .

• apples • beans • carrots
• cauliflowers • celery
• courgettes • cucumbers • kale
• kohl rabi • marrows • onions
• pears • potatoes • salads
• soft fruit • strawberries
• summer cabbage • turnips

Enjoy a crop of mushrooms fresh from your plot.

THREE IDEAS: MAKING MUSHROOMS

❶ Book recycler: soak a paperback. Spread mushroom spawn every thirty pages. Hold the book closed with rubber bands, place the book into a bag and seal. Keep at around 20°C (68°F). Mycelium 'fur' will grow. Spray once or twice a day. After a week the mushrooms will be 5–7cm (2–3in) across and ready to pick.

❷ Raw mushrooms do not freeze so gently fry them; then freeze for up to eight weeks.

❸ To make mushroom compost, buy well-rotted manure or fork fresh horse manure into a heap, packing it down firmly so the manure heats up and add 5 per cent gypsum. Turn the heap every two days for two weeks by forking the cooler manure from the outside until the contents have become dark brown and have a mild, sweet smell.

Grow your own mushrooms

Spawn and a moist, humid atmosphere are the key ingredients in mushroom growing. Sow outside from spring to August on lawns. Lift a section of turf and spread the spores before replacing the turf. Water in. Spread mushroom spores on your compost heap in summer. Harvest in 10–12 weeks.

Indoors, grow mushrooms year round, in any dark place such as a cellar, shed, cupboard or garage, or in a greenhouse in spring or autumn. The ideal temperature is 16°C (61°F). Use 50g (1¾oz) of spores to spawn an area of 0.25sq. m (2¾sq. ft). Yields are best if you use mushroom compost made from straw, horse manure and lime. However, old rotting straw, plain straw and farmyard manure all work. Cover in damp newspaper. After 14–21 days, when white mycelium threads appear, remove the paper to ensure the soil is not too acid. Or you could use half compost and half chalk or lime . . .. Keep moist and wait a month for mushrooms to grow. Aim for three or more crops a year.

What to do

Growing mushrooms on logs involves using dowels that have been impregnated with mushroom mycelium (mushroom spawn). Choose hard woods such as oak, beech, birch, hazel or willow for the logs, which should be 50cm (20in) long and 10–15cm (4–6in) in diameter; they should be kept shaded from direct sunlight and strong winds to stop them drying out. Drill holes 15cm (6in) apart down the length of each log and 7cm (3in) apart around the diameter of the log. Hammer up to fifteen dowels flush into drilled holes, then seal the inoculation holes with wax. Put the logs underground, in a shady place or wrap in a bin bag. Wait 6–18 months. When the mushrooms appear, move the log to a warm, sheltered, moist area in dappled shade such as woodland while it 'fruits'. Logs will be productive for 4–6 years.

Indoors, grow oyster mushrooms in straw in six weeks, all year round. Pour boiling water on bagged straw, leave to cool, drain, sprinkle spawn on the straw and shake. Seal the bag and put in a 18–25°C (64–77°F) environment, such as a boiler cupboard, for a month. Then move the mushroom bag to a 10–15°C (50–59°F) environment for 3–5 days. After that, remove the straw from the bag, place it in a fruiting tray and cover the straw with a perforated fruiting bag, to encourage mushrooms to develop. Place the straw in bright, indirect light, at a temperature of 10–21°C (50–70°F). Spray the straw with water twice a day as the mushrooms begin to develop. Mushrooms should be harvested within ten days, before the caps unfurl and release their spores.

After harvesting the crop, the straw can be soaked in cold water for two hours before returning it to the fruiting tray and repositioning the fruiting bag. Again, place the straw in bright, indirect light at a temperature of 10–21°C (50–70°F). Repeat this process until the straw is exhausted.

Heal yourself with herbs

Using your plot to source medicines gives gardening a whole new dimension. Even the most mundane of plants, and even those that grow by accident, can be useful. Making herbal teas is the standard use for camomile or bergamot, but you can also make ointments, tinctures, poultices and syrups.

If your pot marigolds (*Calendula officinalis*) self-sow and are out of control, make a marigold cream to soothe cuts on your hands caused by pulling them up. Pot marigolds have astringent and anti-inflammatory properties, and the flowers have anti-oxidant properties. When put in pots, products made with pot marigolds make great gifts – and which gardener has not received this classic hand cream for Christmas?

What to do

Take a lump of pure beeswax, weigh it, and measure out about three times its weight in olive oil. Place both wax and oil in a double boiler or a glass bowl over a pan of simmering water so they melt together. When melted, whisk gently and add infused dried marigold petals, gently warming them for 30 minutes or so, then straining. Whisk as it solidifies, then dollop into a pot. Lavender or geranium essential oil also works.

As well as using what you have grown to make creams, it is possible to produce soaps, bath bombs, scrubs, body oils, sprays, talcum powder and masks, and to dye clothes like Tom and Barbara from the 1970s' BBC series *The Good Life*.

For health from the inside out, try making cordial flavoured with what you grow. This may be overplaying a sweet drink's benefits, but anti-oxidant and anti-inflammatory raspberry cordial is full of vitamin C. Use 450g (1lb) sugar and 450ml (15fl. oz) water to make sugar syrup, then add 300g (10oz) raspberries and the juice of two lemons and simmer for five minutes. Stir well, and mash the raspberries up a little. Add two teaspoons tartaric acid, then put the mixture through a strainer and allow to cool. Pour into a bottle and store in the fridge for up to two weeks.

Be your own pharmacist by producing your own tincture. Some say make these on the new moon and strain on the full moon. Put some herbs in a blender. Add alcohol such as vodka to just cover the herbs. Blend well to a soupy consistency and pour into a glass jar. Screw on the lid.

Allow the herbs to settle for a day to see how much liquid is on top. Three-quarters herbs to one-quarter liquid on top is best. Then leave the tincture to brew in the dark for at least four weeks, but do shake the jar at least once a week.

To strain, pour the entire contents of the jar through a strainer and press all liquid out of the soaked herbs with a wooden spoon. Keep the finished tincture sealed as the alcohol will evaporate if left unsealed.

Farm a pharmacy by planting your own herb garden.

THREE IDEAS: HERBAL REMEDIES

❶ Macerated (infused) oil: chop 100g (3.5oz) of herbs. Add 500ml (17fl. oz) olive oil. Place in a bowl over a pan of boiling water for two hours, replacing the water as it boils away. Strain and repeat for one hour, adding fresh herbs. Strain into sterilized glass bottles. Use on the skin as a massage oil or as a healer.

❷ Decoctions: put 15g (½oz) chopped herbs in a pan with 750ml (26fl. oz) water, boil then simmer for twenty minutes. Strain and drink three times a day to aid digestion.

❸ Make rosehip syrup for your joints and skin: halve, de-seed and de-fur 500g (1lb 2oz) rosehips and add 600ml (21fl. oz) water to a pan. Simmer for thirty minutes and add 500g (1lb 1oz) sugar to the strained liquid and boil for three minutes while stirring. Decant into a sterilized bottle.

Warning! Before using herbs in cooking, cosmetics or remedies, check first – some herbs have toxic effects.

August

'The garden is a poor man's apothecary.'
German proverb

124

'You have heard it said that flowers only flourish rightly in the garden of someone that loves them.'

John Ruskin, *Sesame and Lilies*

Let plants sow themselves

This is a high-risk strategy that can save labour and money in the short term, as well as allowing you to be led by nature, which is an attractive, sustainable idea for many gardeners. Any vegetable or herb is suitable, providing you allow it to seed at the end of the growing season and drop seeds to regrow during following seasons. You need to be able to spot what is a seedling and what is a weed from the height of your hoe, because good and bad plants will be all mixed together. The ultimate self-sown plot becomes a kind of edible forest or jungle garden. On this type of low-maintenance plot, onions, berries, bamboo and salad leaves grow under a canopy of self-sown trees, where you may be able to harvest nuts.

What to do

Plants that bolt and set seed such as dill, radishes, rocket and mustards will produce ripe seeds in time for autumn reseeding. Just leave one or two healthy plants to go over.

The general method is that you leave sunflowers, potatoes, poppies, parsnips, artichokes, marigolds and nasturtiums in the ground at the end of the growing season. If you include perennials such as asparagus, fruit trees and bushes and herbs in the list, that is the allotment covered. For maximum gain, shake out the seed heads of your sunflowers or parsnips (for example) in autumn. Transplant seedlings that are too close to each other or are growing too prolifically. Then just weed out what you do not want. Control is vital, so do not let pot marigolds or second-year potatoes, for example, take over.

Allow fallen tomatoes to rot at the end of the season, and they will regrow. Leave a few potatoes in the ground during harvest, to regrow. For tomatoes and potatoes, blight is an issue, so make sure that you dig up everything and throw away diseased plants, if you have seen signs of the disease.

Leave a few pea pods to dry on the plant at the end of the year. They will drop to the ground and regrow. Parsley, coriander and camomile will all go to seed and produce new plants. Scatter scooped pumpkin seed and hope for the best. Store some more seed, in case this technique fails. Do not expect all plants to be true to type.

Plants such as borage and chives can get out of control, so be tough. Cover autumn self-sowers with a cloche to make sure they survive the winter.

> ### THREE IDEAS: SEEDS OF SUCCESS
> ❶ **Collect and swap or sell seed:** packet it up and sell on the internet or stall, alongside other excess seed from magazine cover mounts, et cetera.
> ❷ **Sell your excess** self-sown seedlings at the plot's annual sale or at a car boot sale.
> ❸ **Store seed** surpluses for next year: it lasts longer then you think.

Self-sown allotments are relaxed and unfussy, but they still require upkeep.

Get ready to show off

The produce show is a British institution that enables the humble gardener or cook to have their day in the sun. Growing vegetables for show is not, as many think, about growing the biggest. It is about growing the best example of a vegetable. To be in with the best chance of a rosette, check out the show rules. Is the emphasis on participation and fun, or are there rules and regulations about tying onions, trimming tops and regimented arrangements? If it is a more professional show, think perfection – uniformity of size and colour, ripeness, whether the fruit or veg is reasonably-sized and they have sufficiently long stalks.

Timing your crop to be ripe when the show is due is the toughest part, so know the show date and time, and work backwards. Know what categories are open – they may have changed since last year – and fill in your entry form by the designated time. Choose the best cultivars, so if you need a big onion sow a mammoth variety. Competition root veg requires fine soil, while beans and cucumbers need considerable space in which to grow straight.

Collect your produce when ripe in a trug or similar, so it does not bruise. Clean it carefully as soon as it is picked. Pack in newspaper or cotton wool, and make sure you have plenty of time to arrange your entries before the judges arrive. Take a few extra exhibits in case of an accident. Be absent during judging and take the judges' decision with good grace.

What to do

It is important to know that root veg must have their leaves cut so 7.5cm (3in) of leaf stalk remains. Tie the remaining leaves. Aubergines need to be cut in half. Beans should be podded and uniformly coloured and arranged on a plate. Beetroot: 7.5cm (3in) foliage and 7.5cm (3in) roots. Brassicas: 5cm (2in) stalk. Carrots and parsnips: clean and cut foliage to 7.5cm (3in). Celery: leave a pointed butt end. Courgettes: 15cm (6in) long, 3.5cm (1¼in) diameter. Garlic: 2.5cm (1in) stem. Leeks: leave some outer leaves, uniform in size, and tease out the (cleaned) roots. Lettuce: lift early or late in the day with roots intact and wash. Peas: 2.5cm (1in) stalks. Potatoes: 175–225g (6–8oz) medium-sized, washed specimens are best.

Rhubarb: choose red stalks 7.5cm (3in) long, and cut off the foliage, leaving 7.5cm (3in) from start of the leaf stalks. Tomatoes: stage uniformly coloured fruits on a plate, calyces uppermost.

In fruit categories, pick as near to show time as possible. Cut grapes with a 'T' handle on the end of a bunch. Other fruits need the stalks intact.

For show flowers, take note of the vase sizes where specified; otherwise, ensure the vase size is appropriate to the size of the flowers. Cut for the show in the evening or early morning, when the flowers and foliage are cool. Make a slanting cut at the end of each stalk. Label each item as you go. Plunge in water overnight and leave in a shaded place so that the stems are drawn to the light.

THREE IDEAS: COMPETITIVE STREAK

❶ Popular allotment competition categories are 'Best jam', 'Best chutney' (both made with anything grown on the allotment site) and Best cake with a vegetable ingredient'. If all else fails, ugly/rude veg competitions are good fun if you like that sort of thing. Use cocktail sticks to join ugly veg together to make an ugly veg man. Warped and hairy carrots and parsnips grown in stony soil work well for this.

❷ Read *The Horticultural Show Handbook* (the official RHS guide) for exhaustive tips on the correct way to show produce and put on your own show. Or see http://egvga.eu/information/judging-vegetables.html.

❸ Discreetly trade with neighbours if you are short of one or two items. Do not use the supermarket.

September

'He made two or three peculiar observations; as when shewn the botanical garden, "Is not EVERY garden a botanical garden?"'

James Boswell, *The Life of Samuel Johnson*

1. Collect two cups of blackberries to make four smoothies, picking early in the day.

2. Wash fruits before blending with one of plain yogurt and one of orange juic

MAKING BLACKBERRY SMOOTHIES: STEP BY STEP

3. If you don't have a blender, push fruits through a sieve with a ladle.

4. Add 2–3 tablespoons of honey and tc with blackcurrants and a sprig of mint.

Forage to make smoothies

Foraging may not seem the normal thing to do on a cultivated area such as an allotment plot, but there is plenty of wild food growing on the fringes if you look. In addition, there may well be wild food to forage on the way to and from the plot. Autumn is the traditional time for harvest, when the results of hard graft on the allotment and in the fields are reaped. Mixing foraged with home-grown food has become the most low-carbon and sustainable lifestyle choice. But it could be that the hedgerows near you have been stripped by people taking up nature's bounty during the recession. The reason why gardeners do not grow dandelions or fat hen (*Chenopodium album*) is because they are weeds that spread out of control too easily. Therefore, make controlled 'cultivations' of wild food such as nettles, brambles and other weeds to harvest from your plot.

What to do

Here is a foraged-food 'Top Ten' of plants that should be plentiful in autumn: elder (cordial, cakes, fritters – don't eat them raw as they could be harmful), fat hen (spinach-like weed), nettle (soup), dog rose (jam/tea), dandelion (salad leaves/boiled roots), blackberry (to go with apple pie), cherry (jam/raw), sweet chestnuts (oil/raw), apples (eating or cooking), walnuts and hazelnuts. Rosehips (syrup) and sloes (gin) are also useful wild foods that might be growing near your plot.

For elderflower cordial, mix 1kg (2.2lb) sugar, 1 litre (35fl. oz) boiling water, 20 flower heads, a lemon and 25g (1oz) citric acid.

Blackberries are the classic wild food. They are also a classic weed, prickly, fast-growing and pernicious. But cultivated blackberry varieties such as 'Loch Ness', 'Loch Tay' and 'Loch Maree' are available. Do not pick low-growing blackberries in case they have dog urine on them. Wild crops may not be as sweet as specially bred ones, so may need a bit of help to make them taste nice: for example, mix blackberries with crème fraiche and a bit of muesli. Squeeze through a sieve with the back of a spoon. Then drink.

THREE IDEAS: FRINGE BENEFITS

❶ **Mushrooms**: autumn is the prime mushroom-picking time. Cut with a knife rather than pull them up, to prevent damage to the mycelium, which allows them to regenerate. Use a paper bag to store. Plastic makes fungi sweat. The website www.foragingguide.com offers a guide to identifying the best edible species. Be sure to take expert advice; many poisonous fungi can look very similar to edible species.

❷ **Meat and fish**: fresh roadkill, crabs, angling – all could be sources of wild food.

❸ **Find flavour with your nose**: seaweed, wild garlic, rose petals.

September

Time to sow . . .

DIRECT IN THE PLOT
• winter lettuce

Time to plant . . .
• onion sets • container-grown peach trees • garlic • spring cabbage • strawberries

'What a wond'rous life
is this I lead!
Ripe apples drop about
my head.'

Andrew Marvell, *The Garden*

Time to harvest . . .

- apples • aubergines • beetroot
- blackberries • carrots • chillis
- globe artichokes • marrows
- onions • pears • peas • peppers
- plums • potatoes • pumpkins
- raspberries • squashes
- strawberries • sweetcorn
- tomatoes • turnips

Build a bonfire

The bonfire site on your plot could be just as important as the composting area. Pile thick, thorny material and weeds that are not good for compost on it throughout the year. Bonfire-making used to be a rite of passage, passed on from father to son, as a skill for life. Maybe they are seen as environmentally unfriendly nowadays, but they are not illegal and they are a useful way to get rid of unwanted material – certainly greener than driving rubbish to the tip. Under the Environmental Protection Act, bonfire smoke can be deemed a nuisance, so do not let smoke blow across a road and look out for hedgehogs and whiny neighbours.

Getting started

In an area well away from fences, buildings, trees and plants and out of the wind, pile up wood and other dry material that might burn. Do not add bottles, cans, flammable liquids, plastic, foam, paint or tyres.

Dig a shallow hollow for your fire and put rocks around the side to stop the inferno spreading. Put barbecue charcoal in the middle. Build a teepee shape from twigs, bark, grass and dried leaves over the charcoal. Pile on sticks over the teepee shape, leaving gaps for air. Then lean more sticks and logs around the pile. You can tie the top of the teepee together and then drop in a lit match. Do not use petrol – it explodes.

Have buckets of water, sand and, if you are really paranoid, a fire extinguisher on hand. Put out the fire when you have finished.

Wet wood and leaves equal smoke, so use dry materials for burning. Choose your day. Wind and rain are bad for fires. Bonfire night is a good time. Spring and autumn are ideal seasons after garden clear-ups.

Ash from the bonfire will raise the alkalinity in a compost heap and help compost worms thrive, so they can break down stubborn, acidic kitchen waste and lawn mowings. Sprinkle the potash-rich ash around gooseberries and currant bushes to stop yellowing and browning of leaf edges and to increase fruit yields and quality. Bonfire ash also deters slugs.

THREE IDEAS: BRIGHT SPARKS

❶ A plot is a good place to hold a 5 November **firework celebration**, away from houses and with a dark sky with less light pollution so you can see the display clearly.

❷ **Cook potatoes** wrapped in foil in your bonfire.

❸ **Burn material** treated with pesticides or that has been affected by diseases such as blight, to stop its spread.

Improvise with containers

Unusual containers liven up boring plots, which have often succumbed to the tyranny of raised beds. The risk of using any old junk to plant in is that your plot looks like a tip. But if you get it right, you can create a charming, cheap and quirky, as well as fashionable, plot. Messing about with plant pots that are not plant pots involves very little 'proper' gardening and is good fun. As long as the container holds soil and has drainage holes, you can grow plants in it, almost anywhere. While your plant pot might look eccentric, there is a pleasing simplicity in growing crops in unusual containers.

Getting started

Use your old boots, shopping trolley, toilet pan, sink, bike basket, cheese grater, bucket, bin, car, tyre, teapot or kettle. Think about how the container fits with your style. Lawnmowers and distressed machinery fit well on most plots. A more modern, designed garden needs matching pots, which is something you would expect to see in a kitchen, but rarely come across in a garden. Children love the novelty of Lego, tin-can and sanitary-ware gardens, while adults like not having to spend money on pots. Potato planters are popular, and you can make your own with re-usable carrier bags.

You can increase the number of plants you grow by perching and hanging containers on fences and from trees or, where soil is thin, above roots.

With containers, drainage is key. Cut holes and cover them with kitchen towels or coffee filters. Guttering makes a great container to attach along a fence. Drill holes in it, for drainage. Colanders come with drainage installed. You may want to line them, like a hanging basket, with moss. Another unusual pot that works well as a growing vessel is a pair of cheap plastic shoes. You could also use an old paddling pool for your plants. Again, drainage holes are the key to healthy plants. Drill plenty of them. Herbs go well in these shallow containers. Mint will not spread outside their confines. If your container cannot have holes drilled into it, such as a teacup, grow succulents in it.

> ### THREE IDEAS: COOL CONTAINERS
>
> ❶ Use a broken wheelbarrow as a planter: what else are you going to do with it? Also on a bigger scale, use pallets as improvised raised beds (see page 88)
>
> ❷ Boats make fun containers, especially if they are part of a salty, old-seadog-themed area.
>
> ❸ Old terracotta plant pots are seldom seen now, but were the norm for centuries for a good reason – they make perfect plant receptacles. Dig out vintage pots and give them a new lease of life. The kids can paint them if they look tired.

September

'Our England is a garden that is
full of stately views,
Of borders, beds and shrubberies
and lawns and avenues.'

Rudyard Kipling, *The Glory of the Garden*

....

....

....

....

....

....

....

....

....

....

....

....

....

....

....

....

....

....

....

....

Pumpkin magic

From the fairytale Cinderella's carriage pumpkin to the scary, Halloween's ghoulish gourd and to the garden-show champion, this group of plants produces vegetables that are fun, tasty and impressive. There is nothing more magical than watching a seed grow and transform into a 20kg (44lb) monster – or even a 900kg (142-stone) beast, as grown by world-record holder Ron Wallace (US) in 2012. And there is plenty you can do with these fruits, other than just eat them. In short, look after them by providing plenty of food, water and sun and by positioning the pumpkins on straw or bricks to stop them rotting.

What to do

Sow pumpkin seed in pots from April to June. Plant outside from early summer in manured soil. Alternatively, sow direct in the plot. Each plant needs lots of water and food. Use tomato fertilizer or liquid seaweed extract if it looks a bit jaundiced. Insert a support under the best fruit and get rid of weak plants. Cut the pumpkin when you are ready. Store it in a cool place below 10°C (50°F).

Varieties to try include: 'Atlantic Giant', a 300kg (47-stone) potential record-breaker. Its massive, orange-shelled fruits are ideal for photos of your children or grandchildren sitting on the prize specimen.

'Baby Bear' is good for Halloween carving. To carve, neatly slice off the top (and keep as a lid), remove seeds and begin hollowing with a metal spoon. Draw a design on the face of the pumpkin, not too low, so you can see it. With a short, sharp knife, cut out the design. You can also carve patterns on the skin without cutting all the way through the pumpkin. Place a tea light inside and light with a taper. 'Mammoth' (also known as 'Hundredweight') is a heritage variety. 'Rouge Vif d'Etampes' is the classic Cinderella French pumpkin that will 'take you to the ball'. It is orange-red. Pick small and fry it.

Pumpkin nuts are thin-skinned seeds of (*Cucurbita pepo* var. *styriaca*) pumpkins. Eat the black seeds without peeling, extract salad oil from them (good for strengthening prostate and bladder muscles), then eat the pumpkin flesh.

Squashes are suitable for growing in a small plot. Gourd 'Sweet Dumpling' is especially recommended.

The tastiest allotment recipe is for pumpkin soup. Hollow out the pumpkin with a spoon, which is better than a knife for whittling away at the inside. Cook some chopped onions with oil until they are soft. Then add the pumpkin pieces and some vegetable stock. Season well, and bring to a boil. Then simmer the pumpkin soup. Add cream if you like. Purée the soup with a blender. Sieve and serve, or else freeze it.

You could also fry the pumpkin seeds to add to the soup.

Pumpkins are invaluable for more than Halloween festivities.

THREE IDEAS: ORANGE GIANTS

❶ Try pumpkin chutney: combine a 1.5kg (3lb 4oz) pumpkin (diced), four chopped tomatoes, 500g (1lb 1oz) chopped Bramley apples, one chopped onion, 125g (4oz) dried mixed fruit, 125g (4oz) soft light brown sugar, 2 teaspoons of salt, 1 teaspoon of ground mixed spice, 1 teaspoon ground black pepper, 750ml (26fl. oz) cider vinegar, thyme and tarragon. Boil the ingredients, then simmer for forty-five minutes, before putting in a sterilized jar. Or try pumpkin pie, soup with Parmesan, truffle oil and orange juice or oven-roasted chunks.

❷ Pumpkins make perfect presents. Put them in an autumn allotment gift box.

❸ Swap pumpkin seed: join the European Giant Vegetable Growers Association at http://egvga.webs.com.

October

'The sunlight on the garden
Hardens and grows cold,
We cannot cage the minute
Within its nets of gold,
When all is told
We cannot beg for pardon.'

Louis MacNeice, *The Sunlight on the Garden*

1. Sow seed individually in paper tubes in autumn. Water and place in a cold frame.

2. Place plants outside in March and establish in a sunny spot after frosts f

GROWING SWEET PEAS: STEP BY STEP

3. Support plants with canes arranged into a wigwam and secured with wire or twine.

4. Pick flowers regularly to ensure a long season and to enjoy the scent indoors

Train some sweet peas

If you are nostalgic for all things vintage, and want a plant that is easy to grow and has exciting new varieties, why not choose annual sweet peas (*Lathyrus odoratus*) – cottage-garden favourites?

On your plot, a wigwam of sweet peas adds a bit of colour, scent and interest among the fruit and veg. An early start (between October and January) means stronger plants and better blooms next spring, because the young plants build up healthy root systems during autumn and winter.

Sweet peas are prized for their exquisite scent and colour: old-fashioned, grandiflora heirloom varieties such as 'Cupani' and 'Unique' are back in fashion, because of their superior scent compared with the more modern Spencer varieties. However, they have smaller blooms.

Perennial sweet peas (*L. latifolius*) are another option, but they have a limited colour range – white, rose and pink – and not much scent. So it is best to stick to the annual varieties, and the nostalgic smell of the vintage bloom will be your reward in June.

Getting started

Sow each seed in an 8cm (3in) pot, 6 to 8 in a 15cm (6in) pot, or sow more densely in a seed tray to thin later. Some growers swear by sowing seed in cardboard toilet-roll centres, one seed in each tube. Do not nick or soak the seed: it is a fiddly job that will not make much difference to germination. Use multipurpose potting compost and cover the seed with a layer 1cm (½in) deep or less. Water with a fine-rose watering can. Place in a cold frame or cold greenhouse and protect against mice and slugs. Germination should take place after two weeks.

The later into autumn you sow, the more likely seed is to need a bit of heat, perhaps on a windowsill. Move back to the greenhouse or cold frame when the seed germinates so the seedlings do not get leggy: pinch out the tips for more side shoots. Place pots outside for a week in March, then plant out in a sunny spot after the last frosts. Put two or three plants in one hole and space holes 15cm (6in) apart for a full display.

A wigwam using canes tied together with string is pretty, but takes effort. Training single plants up a cane works well for a quality bloom, while netting against a wall is effective, too, to create a temporary screen: use wire rings to hold unruly plants in place. If you miss the autumn sowing slot, or cannot face cosseting your plants through winter, sow direct into soil in spring, or buy plug plants.

THREE IDEAS: SWEET SUCCESS

❶ **Cut your own** fragrant sweet peas for flower arranging.
❷ **Use your sweet-pea wigwam** frame for edible peas.
❸ Enter a vase of your finest sweet peas in a **flower show**.

October

Time to sow . . .

DIRECT IN THE PLOT
- broad beans

Time to plant . . .

- onion sets
- garlic • spring cabbage

Time to harvest . . .

- apples • beetroot • cabbage
- carrots • French beans • pears
- potatoes • runner beans

'For you, little gardener and lover of trees, I have only a small gift. Here is set G for Galadriel, but it may stand for garden in your tongue.'

J.R.R. Tolkien, *Fellowship of the Ring*

Make your own compost

Compost is organic matter that has decomposed. Once well rotted, use it as soil conditioner and fertilizer, and to bulk up soil with humus. You can make leafmould by putting leaves in a bag and waiting. Better still, use water, air and carbon- and nitrogen-rich materials to make your garden compost. You need an equal amount of dry, brown material full of carbon and green, damp material full of nitrogen. Shred the plant matter, add water and turn the heap regularly with a fork to aerate it. Worms are good to break up the material. Good bacteria are the key – but you will not be able to see them. If the heap is warm inside, the bacteria are working.

What to do

Some councils sell cheap compost bins. Put your brown and green waste in one of these containers, and pull it out of the bottom when it has thoroughly rotted. Alternatively, store the compost in a box-based system.

Any green matter (apart from perennial weeds) is suitable for your compost bin. Grass and young material get the compost going. Also suitable are vegetable peelings, old tea leaves and coffee grounds. For the carbon-rich brown matter, paper and cardboard works, as does old straw from pets. Leaves and ash are OK. Woody bits rot slowly, so break them up. You could urinate on your heap to move things along – the nitrogen helps. Avoid meat-based foods (which attract vermin) and diseased plant material. Burn blight-ridden potatoes and tomatoes; never compost them.

For leafmould compost you need a wire cage to encase your leaf pile. Or put leaves in bin bags, tie them up and make holes in the bags. After a year, the leaves should have crumbled, and you can spread them on your soil. Old leafmould (of two or more years) is good for seed sowing. Mix it with garden compost, sharp sand and garden soil to make potting compost.

To get pea or bean seeds off to a good start, incorporate a layer of old kitchen waste in their trench. Procure the kitchen waste from the local pub. Source other compostable material from farms and riding schools.

THREE IDEAS: WASTE NOT, WANT NOT

❶ Mulch your plot with newspaper soaked in wallpaper paste.

❷ Four pallets strung together to form a box shape make a good compost bin, while for a leafmould bin you need four stakes, at the corners, wrapped with chicken wire to make a square cage.

❸ Buy a wormery: this is a container in which worms are kept. Feed them with kitchen waste. They will convert the waste into compost. Wormeries and worms to fill them are readily available to buy. Try www.wormery.co.uk or www.wigglywigglers.co.uk.

A rich and varied compost heap is the basis for a fertile plot.

Get fitter by gardening

Gardening is good exercise in itself, but it is easy to become complacent by thinking that eating home-grown produce and doing some digging make you fit. Going to the gym costs a lot more than gardening, so use your plot to its full advantage as an exercise centre. You could just garden to maintain your physical fitness, but there are fat gardeners, so perhaps a bit more intensive exercise on your plot might benefit your health.

Get started

You can burn 600–700 calories in three hours' gardening, or in one hour's intensive gardening. Gardening is good because you are on soft surfaces such as grass or soil, rather than jarring your knees on concrete. Shuttle running on grass or soil prevents joint shock caused by harder surfaces. Mowing, raking, barrowing and digging are good exercises.

Because the body turns, these exercises are better for muscles than using fixed-weight machines in the gym, which work muscles only one way. Squat when weeding to exercise glutes (buttock muscles). Hoe, strim and fork compost into a barrow for abs ('six-pack' muscles). Push a laden barrow for biceps and shoulders. Carry watering cans. Twenty minutes on each activity is ideal. Bend the knees to avoid back strain.

Build a whole circuit for more intensive training. I would suggest a minute of each of these: trampoline, shuttle run, pull-ups on a branch, press-ups leaning on your garden bench, lifting two full watering cans – one in each hand – and pushing a full barrow for a shuttle. Then do it again.

Further pastimes for your plot include using a strip of artificial grass for putting/cricket net/croquet/skittles, crazy golf, yoga or t'ai chi in the peace of your plot, fly-casting practice, giant garden games (draughts, chess, Twister, quoits, boules), a bouncy castle/trampoline or swingball. You could also tie an abseiling rope on a tree you can climb, hang a punchbag from a branch, set up a climbing wall with foot- and handholds or, if it gets wet, you could mud-wrestle in the mire.

> ### THREE IDEAS: ALLOTMENT ACTIVITIES
>
> ❶ For more leisurely pursuits, a **sunbathing platform** is an inviting idea for the summer.
> ❷ Use the plot to land your **model aircraft**, or fly your kite, or sail your model boat in your pond.
> ❸ **Dog agility classes**: set up kids' playtunnels, hurdles and a ring of fire to use when exercising your dog.

October

....
....
....
....
....
....
....
....
....
....
....
....
....
....
....
....

'To sit in the shade on a perfect day and look upon verdure is the most perfect refreshment.'

Jane Austen, *Mansfield Park*

Do you really need to dig?

Double digging is one of the most strenuous types of cultivation, and there is a debate in gardening about whether digging to the depth of two spade blades ('spits'), or even digging at all, is worth the effort. There is a hands-on satisfaction in digging and connecting with the earth that you can only really get from gardening. Spadework is good exercise, and well-cultivated soil is easy to use when growing plants. On poor or heavy soil, double dig every 3–5 years; digging in air and organic matter is important, for example, on compacted soils or new plots that used to be lawns. Some plants such as asparagus need deep topsoil.

Dig in autumn before the soil gets too wet, because, if the soil gets waterlogged, its structure goes and not much grows. And cultivate before the ground freezes in winter and becomes unworkable.

What to do

In double digging you turn not only the topsoil, but also a spit of subsoil that is then worked through with well-rotted manure. Keep the subsoil and topsoil separate. Remove the soil from the upper and lower spits of the first trench and from the upper spit of the second trench, placing it aside on the ground in three separate, clearly marked piles. The soil can then be transferred from the lower spit of the second trench to the base of the first trench, after manure has been added to it, and from the upper spit of the third trench to the top of the first. This ensures that the topsoil and subsoil remain separate. Continue digging trenches in the same way, until you reach the end of the bed, where soil saved from the first trench can be used to fill the appropriate layers in the final trench.

Some gardeners say do not dig at all. It ruins the soil structure and encourages weeds. But many people like digging. On the other hand, undug soil, managed under the no-dig method, retains moisture well and is firm but not compacted. Lay compost on top and allow it to work down. This works best in raised beds. Undisturbed soil life can help fertility, as undisturbed capillary channels are left to do their work. The lack of clods and weeds are advantages of not digging. Turning over the soil can bring weed seeds to the surface. Also, digging can damage mycorrhizal fungi in the soil, which help plant roots to find nutrients. However, beet and brassica plants do not use mycorrhizal associations to improve rooting so are not so damaged by digging.

> **THREE IDEAS: DON'T DIG…**
>
> ❶ **Rake the soil** to a fine tilth just before sowing in spring.
> ❷ **Hoe weeds** rather than dig them out.
> ❸ **Try an adze** to till the soil.

November

'There were apples that rivalled rubies; pears of topaz tint, some purple as the amethyst, others blue and brilliant as the sapphire; an emerald here, and now a golden drop that gleamed like the yellow diamond of Genghis Khan.'

Benjamin Disraeli, *Sybil*

Build a pond

A pond is a boon for attracting all manner of wildlife to your plot. As the idea is to create more interest in your plot – not to introduce a potential hazard – you should make sure that children will not be able to play near the water unattended. Also avoid overhanging trees, because they will drop leaves into the pond.

Get started

Make your pond site as big as you can, given any restrictions of size on your plot, and mark it out. Dig at least 75cm (30in) deep in the centre to stop it freezing in winter. A good design is a saucer shape with gently sloping edges so animals such as hedgehogs can get in and out.

The pond will need to be lined. The best liner is butyl rubber. It is wise to buy a piece that is bigger than you think you will need. You should aim to have a 30cm (12in) overlap around the edge of the pond. (Alternatively, you can buy a preformed, rigid pond liner, for which you will need to dig a matching-shaped hole.)

Dig out the centre of the pond, then either create shelves at the sides or give the pond sloping edges. Remove sharp stones and compact the soil. Then cover the base with 3cm (1¼in) of builders' sand and maybe some carpet, underlay or old newspaper over the area to help stop the pond liner puncturing. Spread out the liner over the prepared pond base and secure the edge with bricks. Place a thin layer of soil over the liner and gradually add water while pulling the edges of the liner so that it fits neatly over the contours of the pond. Trim the liner, edge with turf and plant (in the spring or summer) when the soil has settled. Wait for amphibians, pond insects and birds to arrive.

Introduce aquatic plants to enrich the pond water with oxygen, support beneficial bacteria that eat the debris and give frogs and dragonflies somewhere to live. Recommended water plants include: spiked water milfoil (*Myriophyllum spicatum*), water starwort (*Callitriche hermaphroditica*, syn. *C. autumnalis*), miniature water lily (*Nymphaea*) and water soldier (*Stratiotes aloides*).

Add fish, but not koi carp, which chew water-lily roots, leaving a plant void in which algae can establish. To make matters worse, koi waste raises nitrate levels in the water, adding to the green-soup effect.

> ### THREE IDEAS: WATER WAYS
> ❶ **Keep carp** for food.
> ❷ **Harvest rainwater** to top up your pond.
> ❸ **Build a pond** for amphibians in a pot or hand basin, or raise on to a table top.

November

....

....

....

Time to sow . . .
UNDER CLOCHES
• beans • peas

Time to plant . . .
• fruit trees and bushes
• garlic

....

....

....

....

....

....

....

....

....

....

....

....

....

....

....

....

....

Time to harvest . . .

- Brussels sprouts • carrots
- cauliflowers • celeriac • celery
- Jerusalem artichokes • kale
- kohl rabi • leeks • parsnips
- salsify • scorzonera
- winter cabbage

'Your first job is to prepare the soil. The best tool for this is your neighbor's motorized garden tiller. If your neighbor does not own a garden tiller, suggest that he buy one.'

Dave Barry, *Insane City*

Boost your productivity

Success in growing serious amounts of veg is often achieved by using raised beds and greenhouses, and by lots of work. The key is to split your plot so you have manageable chunks. Think about what you want a lot of and concentrate on that. If you have too many crops, it could be that you have spread your workload too wide.

Getting started

To get the most out of the season, start early by growing seedlings in a greenhouse or indoors. One idea is to start seedlings off in teabags, or just use conventional seed trays with or without individual cells. Then plant out into a bought or a home-made cold frame created from a salvaged window laid on four bales of straw. Better still, use a polytunnel to extend the season and so increase production. To make one, bend over and wedge 2.5cm (1in) PVC plumbers' pipes into metal tubes driven into the ground and spaced 1m (39in) apart. Cover in plastic sheeting.

Prepare your plot by incorporating lots of well-rotted manure and green manures to add nitrogen. Think about crop rotation. After green manuring with leguminous or brassica crops, do not grow legumes or brassicas in the same place the following season, to avoid disease and to ensure the correct nutrients are available.

If you do not want to sow seed, and do not mind a bit more expense, buy plug plants, which will provide a flying start to the growing season.

One of the best crops to give you a maximum return on the space is courgettes, as long as they are well fed and watered. Prepare the soil by digging in well-rotted manure. Grow the seed on in a greenhouse until you can plant them out, or buy plug plants

and plant out. But beware of slugs. Nematodes are a good, green way to see off these pests. These microscopic worms feed on molluscs when watered into the soil. However, you will need to water daily, or failing that at least three times a week, for the nematodes to stay alive. Pinch out extraneous leaves and spare fruit on the courgette plants.

Runner beans are also good croppers and are very reliable. From late May to the end of June sow runner bean seed 5cm (2in) deep and 20cm (8in) apart. Or sow in 10cm (4in) pots at the end of April indoors and plant out at the end of May 20cm (8in) apart. Sow a double row with the two rows 50cm (20in) apart and make a ridge support of bamboo canes, looking like an old-fashioned ridge tent, to train them up.

Garlic is expensive to buy but cheap to grow, and does not take up much space, so try planting cloves in spring and waiting for bulbs in late summer.

Tomatoes are a good idea, too. There is a wide range of interesting shapes and sizes – do not just go for round ones. Grow tomatoes in a growbag, and feed with home-made comfrey 'tea'. To make this, soak comfrey leaves in water for four weeks.

Do not bother to grow potatoes, carrots, cabbage or onions, because they are cheap to buy.

THREE IDEAS: FEED THE BIRDS

❶ Make your own **bird-food cupcakes** by mixing one-third melted suet, with two-thirds seeds and chopped dried fruit. Allow to dry, then hang up for the birds.

❷ A **feeding station**, including a water source made from artificial materials, is just as likely to attract birds as a more rustic-looking, home-made set-up.

❸ **Feed all year round**. Birds will eat more insects in the summer, so make your allotment a wildlife haven by planting (pesticide-free) food plants; include log piles, compost heaps, mown and unmown grass, fruit trees, berry-rich hedges and ponds.

Create a haven for birds

In many allotments, foxes, badgers, deer, squirrels, moles and rodents are not welcome. However, gardeners do love wild birds, but not all of course – seagulls, pigeons and parakeets get a bad press. Starlings, pheasants and magpies can also be unwanted guests.

Smaller, more vulnerable feathered friends have a £200 million a year industry built around them, as allotment-holders seek to attract, feed and keep alive robins, tits, finches and other songbirds. Complicating matters is the problem that by feeding the birds you can attract squirrels and rodents, so how do you bring in the birds you want to see rather than the creatures you want to avoid?

Getting started

Encourage smaller birds by providing the food they like in caged feeders that big birds cannot access. Wood pigeons, for example, are not agile enough to eat from hanging feeders. If you hang a range of feeders, other birds will not be scared off by flocks of greenfinches.

If you want to attract specific birds, you need to feed them the foods that they prefer: for example, greenfinches, nuthatches, tits, siskins and woodpeckers particularly like peanuts. Buy good-quality ones and hang in a feeder, because whole peanuts could choke a bird. A fungus can contaminate old peanuts with aflatoxins, which are toxic to birds and humans. Robins and dunnocks like peanut granules.

Tits and woodpeckers enjoy eating from coconut halves, while jays love acorns. Robins and blue tits relish fat balls, which are the cheap 'loss leader' in the wild bird food market. Blue tits also like mealworms – live food

is becoming more popular to buy for birds, particularly during the breeding season. Provide the mealworms in covered dishes so they do not drown.

Nuthatches feed on shelled hazelnuts, while linnets and chaffinches like marijuana seed, of the non-narcotic strain. Nyger seed is popular with goldfinches. Sunflower seed is great, with sunflower hearts perfect for birds that cannot crack the seed coats. Individual seeds are better than mixed ones.

Chaffinches prefer feed scattered on the ground. Many gardeners fear attracting rodents by putting food on the ground, but more of an issue to many gardeners are grey squirrels, which are greedy, agile and take bird food to store. Squirrel-proof feeders and 'baffle' barriers on bird-table legs are the answer in many cases.

Cats are a much worse problem, killing about 55 million UK songbirds annually. A dog, sprays and electrical devices deter felines.

One of the best ways to bring wildlife to your garden is to provide food for the birds.

November

'A garden always has
a point.'

Elizabeth Hoyt, *The Raven Prince*

Gardening by the moon

Gardening at night is more than just using a torch to toil by, because you did not have time during daylight. There is something that frees you from the conventions of society when you garden at a time you are not supposed to. And gardening and planting by the moon is a system that can produce bigger crops of better-tasting veg. However, you need a moon timetable to tap into the energy cycles of the moon and harness its lunar energy.

Biodynamics is favoured by Prince Charles. The philosophy was founded in 1924 by Austrian teacher and philosopher Rudolf Steiner, who adopted holistic principles and took into account the condition of the cosmos. Plants get energy from the sun, but also are affected by the moon, just like the tides.

The moon's pull causes high tides twice a month, a day after full and new moons. This leads to rainfall peaking three or four days after full and new moons, say moon gardeners. You should plant pumpkins three days before full moon, according to native American tradition, which also says the 'three sisters' of sweetcorn, pumpkins and beans should be planted together to support each other.

Methods unique to the biodynamic approach include a closed system of composting from your own animals and the use of fermented herbal and mineral preparations as compost additives and field sprays, as well as following the astronomical sowing and planting calendar.

What to do

Biodynamics is certified by Demeter (www.biodynamic.org.uk). This method of organic gardening has three main elements: using horn manure (BD 500) and horn silica (BD 501) as field sprays; using five herbal preparations, including yarrow, valerian and dandelion, on the compost heap; following a biodynamic calendar for planting and doing other jobs in the garden. Horn manure works in the root zone and horn silica is active in the area of light and plant growth.

You can make horn manure by filling a cow's horn with cow manure and burying it in the soil in autumn. Dig it up the following spring and dilute the manure at one teaspoon to 50 litres (11 gallons) of water. Alternatively, fill a 1m- (3ft-) deep, brick-lined 'cow-pat pit' in the garden with fresh cow manure that is treated with specially fermented compost preparations such as crushed egg and basalt dust. Cover the pit with a wet sack and wooden boards to keep out the weather. After three months, add a few grammes of the manure to 75 litres (16½ gallons) of water, stir, and use as a spray.

More options include packing camomile blossom in cow intestines or oak bark in animal skulls and burying them. There is not much scientific proof for these ideas, but working with the occult on your allotment may appeal if you are bored with the humdrum digging, planting, weeding and watering routine of gardening.

THREE IDEAS: AFTER DARK

❶ **Astronomy in your plot**: works well in the peace and dark. Some plants smell more potent at dusk – night phlox, evening stock, moonflower, datura, lilies, petunia and nicotiana.

❷ **Make a semaphore station or lighthouse**: build a tower to signal to fellow allotment holders. You could also add a sundial, thermometer, barometer and rain gauge to make a weather station.

❸ **Experiment with photography** and lights to gain a new perspective on your plot.

December

'The garden is never dead;
growth is always going on.'

Henry Ellacombe, *In My Vicarage Garden*

Plant a herb garden

Herbs are about smell and touch, but look attractive too, although you should not allow them to flower as this detracts from the taste. They fall mostly into two distinctive groups, culinary and aromatic, although lavender is usually used for its perfume but can also flavour baking.

Put herbs in the bath, in hot drinks, in room fragrances, in medicines and, of course, eat them raw and cooked.

There are annual herbs such as basil, coriander and sweet marjoram; perennials such as mint and fennel, and bushy perennials such as rosemary, lavender, thyme and sage.

Map out where you plan to plant your herbs, thinking about how big they will become when designing spacing. A sunny spot works best. Pots, hanging baskets or raised beds with grit dug in may work better for rosemary, lavender and thyme, which suffer when their roots get wet. Or mix them between other plants, where they work well as aphid repellants.

What to plant

Lots of herbs are difficult to start off: for example, parsley is a struggle, as are basil and tarragon. You are better off buying a supermarket parsley plant and keeping it on your windowsill. Divide the herb and plant each piece separately into the ground.

Herbs that you can grow from seed directly into your plot include wild rocket (which is sown from April to August and is great as peppery salad leaves) and coriander (sown from March to May as a curry garnish). Borage flowers are said to drive out melancholy, which we all need. Bees love them too, and watching bees buzzing for a while can lift the blues.

In spring, direct-sow borage, which is a good companion plant for tomatoes, squashes and strawberries. Also sow chervil and dill direct, from March to August, as they are difficult to transplant.

Mint spreads fast, so restrict root growth by planting it in a sunken bucket or plastic pot with holes. The woodier herbs such as rosemary, thyme and sage are better planted as young plug plants, rather than from seed.

Herbal 'Earl Grey' tea is a blend that you can make yourself at home. Commercial Earl Grey tea incorrectly uses the citrus fruit bergamot instead of the herb bergamot (*Monarda didyma*) (grow by direct sowing in spring). Use one teaspoon black tea combined with three teaspoons fresh bergamot leaves cut first thing in the morning, when its oil is most concentrated. Pour on boiling water and steep for five minutes before pouring yourself a well-earned drink.

A patchwork of lavender, marigolds, chives, thyme and other herbs.

December

Time to sow . . .

INDOORS
- cauliflowers • lettuce • onions
- radish • summer cabbage
- turnips

Time to force . . .
- chicory • seakale

Time to plant . . .
- fruit trees and bushes

THREE IDEAS: HERB HELP

① **Gather a bunch** of lemon balm, rosemary, lemon verbena, lavender and mint, and place it inside a muslin herb bag to hang under the hot tap and infuse the bath with scent.

② **Make herb tea**: use five fresh leaves, a 5cm (2in) sprig or two teaspoons of dried herb per cup. Crush the herb, put it in a cup and pour over hot water. While the tea brews, cover the cup to stop evaporation. Peppermint is good for digestion and lemon balm cheers you up.

③ **Grow herbs indoors** hydroponically using a premixed nutrient solution for plants that are grown without soil and often under lights. You will need to buy a hydroponic system; try www.growell.co.uk.

Time to harvest . . .

- Brussels sprouts • carrots
- cauliflowers • celeriac • celery
- chicory • endive • Jerusalem artichokes • kale • kohl rabi
- leeks • lettuce • parsnips
- perpetual spinach • salsify
- scorzonera • spinach
- swedes • turnips • winter cabbage • winter radish

THREE IDEAS: BRANCHING OUT

1 Plant a pot-grown **Christmas tree** on your plot.

2 **Tree surgery** is a good skill to learn. You will need safety equipment and training, as well as a chainsaw.

3 **Orchard grants**: research these to see whether you might qualify, on www.orchardnetwork.org.uk/content/grants-fundraising.

Grow a mini-orchard

Make your allotment orchard area more than a place to produce fruit. Edible landscaping using fruit trees and vines, as well as nut trees, is often found in community areas, which lend themselves to shared work for relaxation – and lounging among the trees in the shade. All plot-holders can then enjoy the orchard changing throughout the season, watching trees transform from leafless skeletons to producing blossom, leaves, fruit and autumn colours.

The ideal place on the plot is a neglected fringe area, which may already have fruit trees growing on it. This area could also be designated a wildlife space, but will succeed as such only if you leave it well alone.

If your fruit trees are not self-fertile, to ensure a good crop you may need two trees of each type – especially with apples, pears and cherries.

What to do

Plant young fruit trees, which are usually two trees grafted together by nurseries for optimum performance. Grow varieties not available at the supermarket, such as heritage apples like 'Deddington Pippin' or favourites such as 'Bramley's Seedling', 'Cox's Orange Pippin' and 'Egremont Russet'. Choose a dwarf apple rootstock (any tree labelled 'M27' or 'M9') so you can easily reach the fruit. Some fruit trees are trained into cordons, espaliers or fans, so take up less space. Plant these to run along a sheltered, sunny fence.

Trees can be bought either in a container or bare-root. Plant bare-root trees from late autumn to early winter; soak the roots before planting. Container-grown trees can be planted at any time of year except when frosty or if the soil is too dry or too wet. Place your tree in a sunny and sheltered site. Dig a hole a third wider than the tree's roots and to the same depth. Ensure the tree is planted at the same depth as it was previously growing, by checking the soil mark on the

trunk. Stake the tree (until it becomes established), water and mulch over the root zone. Use a spiral tree guard or wire-mesh barrier to protect the trunk from rabbits.

If you want to grow your tree in a container, half fill a large tub with soil-based potting compost and place the tree on top. Fill the tub with more soil up to the soil mark on the tree's trunk, and water well. Feed and water the tree regularly.

An orchard can be part of a permaculture. Such a system of permanent agriculture involves an integrated, sustainable way of growing with nature. For example, all the mulch for the orchard could be provided by your prunings. The mulch could be inoculated with edible fungus to help break it down, and later manure spread to help break down all the orchard litter and minimize disease. Conserving water, growing a diversity of crops and using your own chicken's manure in a nutrient cycle are other aspects of permaculture.

A mini-orchard provides more than just fruit.

Grow truffles and gourmet nuts

Truffles (not the chocolate type) are a type of mushroom that grows on the roots of hazel and oak trees throughout Europe. Food-lovers adore these intensely flavoured delicacies as well as fresh hazelnuts, but they are very expensive to buy. Making money from your allotment while providing habitats and shelter for wildlife is therefore a golden ticket for many plot-holders. One way to do this is to plant truffle trees, which are hazel trees that have been inoculated with the truffle fungus.

Awareness of these fascinating native fungi is growing quickly and so is interest in truffle trees. Home growers range from people who have a couple of trees in a back garden to those who have filled their whole allotment.

What to do

Hazel trees (*Corylus avellana*) are hardy, native plants, suitable for any plot size, because they react well to pruning. You can use oaks too, but they may grow too big for most allotment plots. Grow lavender among the trees. Allotments in cool-temperate regions should have a suitable climate, and the soil should ideally be pH 7.3–7.9. Late winter or early spring is a good time to plant young, inoculated hazel trees.

Buy 30cm (12in) saplings and plant them densely, or your truffles may suffer from under-colonization. Truffles do not expect too much water or fertilizer, and they should be produced three or four years after planting.

Fresh truffles are harvested from July to November. They grow just under the soil's surface, and finding them is half the fun. Traditionally, pigs or dogs dug them up. Truffles can be used to flavour egg dishes, pasta, fish, honey and oils.

A typical hazel tree should produce 1kg (2.2lb) of truffles per year after 4–6 years. They can live for 50 years and are also great wildlife trees.

The hazel trees used to cultivate truffles will also produce edible nuts.

THREE IDEAS: TRUFFLE TIPS

❶ Combine your nuts and truffles in **truffle risotto**. If you have never tried truffles, then a good introduction is to try some truffle-infused olive oil by drizzling it on mashed potato or scrambled eggs.
❷ **Coppice the trees**: regular cutting leads to better growth.
❸ Send your dog to truffle-hunting **dog school**: see www.plantationsystems.com/dog-training-school; www.gbita.com.

Truffles are a delicacy and can grow on the roots of specially prepared hazel trees.

December

'Did perpetual happiness in
the Garden of Eden maybe
get so boring that eating
the apple was justified?'

Chuck Palahniuk, *Survivor*

Guerrilla garlanding in winter

There is little point in attempting to grow things in the middle of winter. You cannot even dig, because the soil is sodden or frozen, and your plot will already have been topdressed with tons of manure. Rather than retire in front of the fire with seed catalogues for next year, staring and shivering at the bare bones of your garden, or drawing a plan of how you want your plot to look in the bright, fresh season, think about your gardening manifesto, or style. It could be having no plant or object made in a certain part of the world. Think of the plot as your blank canvas, in which you can turn nothing into something by introducing a fresh approach on life outdoors.

Becoming fashionable again are indoor Christmas plants such as Christmas cacti, hyacinths (plant bulbs in September/October), amaryllis, poinsettias and – the uncoolest of all – the polyanthus basket. Give them as presents to subvert your friends' idea of cool – unless they throw them away, of course.

What to do

More whimsically, decorate street, park, a fellow plot-holder's or your own trees (preferably conifers) with tinsel (or home-made baubles and fairies) as a form of anarchic, guerrilla garlanding to brighten up everyone's day. This is a good alternative to cutting down a tree to keep inside your house.

Make wreaths, too, and hang them on postboxes. Flickr, Facebook and tweet the results. Harvest pine cones to spray and make into Christmas decorations. Do the same with holly, ivy and mistletoe.

Of course, guerrilla gardening is fun all year round. Why not plant edible crops in council beds, on roundabouts and verges? Before winter hits, plant bulbs where they will spring up and surprise passers-by. You do not have to worry about maintenance – if it works that is fine, and if it does not it is not your problem.

You can, of course, grow your own Christmas dinner (well, some of it, such as the sprouts, parsnips, nuts and potatoes). Brassicas overwinter, as do root veg, artichokes, kohl rabi, winter radish, salsify, scorzonera and autumn-sown beans and peas.

THREE IDEAS: WINTER ACTIVITY

❶ Cover your delicate plants with fleece to protect them from frost. The ghostly apparitions you create are great to spook children.

❷ Feed the birds: there is a whole art to this (see page 166). Squash mistletoe berries into apple-tree branches to grow your own parasitic kissing plant.

❸ Make a snowman: add a nose made from one of your home-grown carrots. Try making a kangaroo or squirrel snow animal, or a snow throne or igloo.

Plans

Useful contacts

November

UNDER CLOCHES
- beans • peas

Time to plant . . .
- fruit trees and bushes
- garlic

Build a pond

A pond is a boon for attracting all manner of wildlife to your plot. As the idea is to create more interest in your plot – not to introduce a potential hazard – you should make sure that children will not be able to play near the water unattended. Also avoid overhanging trees, because they will drop leaves into the pond.

Get started

Make your pond site as big as you can, given any restrictions of size on your plot, and mark it out. Dig at least 75cm (30in) deep in the centre to stop it freezing in winter. A good design is a saucer shape with gently sloping edges so animals such as hedgehogs can get in and out.

The pond will need to be lined. The best liner is butyl rubber. It is wise to buy a piece that is bigger than you think you will need. You should aim to have a 30cm (12in) overlap around the edge of the pond. (Alternatively, you can buy a preformed, rigid pond liner, for which you will need to dig a matching-shaped hole.)

Dig out the centre of the pond, then either create shelves at the sides or give the pond sloping edges. Remove sharp stones and compact the soil. Then cover the base with 3cm (1¼in) of builders' sand and maybe some carpet, underlay or old newspaper over the area to help stop the pond liner puncturing. Spread out the liner over the prepared pond base and secure the edge with bricks. Place a thin layer of soil over the liner and gradually add water while pulling the edges of the liner so that it fits neatly over the contours of the pond. Trim the liner, edge with turf and plant (in the spring or summer) when the soil has settled. Wait for amphibians, pond insects and birds to arrive.

Introduce aquatic plants to enrich the pond water with oxygen, support beneficial bacteria that eat the debris and give frogs and dragonflies somewhere to live. Recommended water plants include: spiked water milfoil (*Myriophyllum spicatum*), water starwort (*Callitriche hermaphroditica*, syn. *C. autumnalis*), miniature water lily (*Nymphaea*) and water soldier (*Stratiotes aloides*).

Add fish, but not koi carp, which chew water-lily roots, leaving a plant void in which algae can establish. To make matters worse, koi waste raises nitrate levels in the water, adding to the green-soup effect.

> ## THREE IDEAS: WATER WAYS
> ❶ **Keep carp** for food.
> ❷ **Harvest rainwater** to top up your pond.
> ❸ **Build a pond** for amphibians in a pot or hand basin, or raise on to a table top.

Guerrilla garlanding in winter

There is little point in attempting to grow things in the middle of winter. You cannot even dig, because the soil is sodden or frozen, and your plot will already have been topdressed with tons of manure. Rather than retire in front of the fire with seed catalogues for next year, staring and shivering at the bare bones of your garden, or drawing a plan of how you want your plot to look in the bright, fresh season, think about your gardening manifesto, or style. It could be having no plant or object made in a certain part of the world. Think of the plot as your blank canvas, in which you can turn nothing into something by introducing a fresh approach on life outdoors.

Becoming fashionable again are indoor Christmas plants such as Christmas cacti, hyacinths (plant bulbs in September/October), amaryllis, poinsettias and – the uncoolest of all – the polyanthus basket. Give them as presents to subvert your friends' idea of cool – unless they throw them away, of course.

What to do

More whimsically, decorate street, park, a fellow plot-holder's or your own trees (preferably conifers) with tinsel (or home-made baubles and fairies) as a form of anarchic, guerrilla garlanding to brighten up everyone's day. This is a good alternative to cutting down a tree to keep inside your house.

Make wreaths, too, and hang them on postboxes. Flickr, Facebook and tweet the results. Harvest pine cones to spray and make into Christmas decorations. Do the same with holly, ivy and mistletoe.

Of course, guerrilla gardening is fun all year round. Why not plant edible crops in council beds, on roundabouts and verges? Before winter hits, plant bulbs where they will spring up and surprise passers-by. You do not have to worry about maintenance – if it works that is fine, and if it does not it is not your problem.

You can, of course, grow your own Christmas dinner (well, some of it, such as the sprouts, parsnips, nuts and potatoes). Brassicas overwinter, as do root veg, artichokes, kohl rabi, winter radish, salsify, scorzonera and autumn-sown beans and peas.

THREE IDEAS: WINTER ACTIVITY

❶ Cover your delicate plants with fleece to protect them from frost. The ghostly apparitions you create are great to spook children.

❷ Feed the birds: there is a whole art to this (see page 166). Squash mistletoe berries into apple-tree branches to grow your own parasitic kissing plant.

❸ Make a snowman: add a nose made from one of your home-grown carrots. Try making a kangaroo or squirrel snow animal, or a snow throne or igloo.

Plans

Gardening by the moon

Gardening at night is more than just using a torch to toil by, because you did not have time during daylight. There is something that frees you from the conventions of society when you garden at a time you are not supposed to. And gardening and planting by the moon is a system that can produce bigger crops of better-tasting veg. However, you need a moon timetable to tap into the energy cycles of the moon and harness its lunar energy.

Biodynamics is favoured by Prince Charles. The philosophy was founded in 1924 by Austrian teacher and philosopher Rudolf Steiner, who adopted holistic principles and took into account the condition of the cosmos. Plants get energy from the sun, but also are affected by the moon, just like the tides.

The moon's pull causes high tides twice a month, a day after full and new moons. This leads to rainfall peaking three or four days after full and new moons, say moon gardeners. You should plant pumpkins three days before full moon, according to native American tradition, which also says the 'three sisters' of sweetcorn, pumpkins and beans should be planted together to support each other.

Methods unique to the biodynamic approach include a closed system of composting from your own animals and the use of fermented herbal and mineral preparations as compost additives and field sprays, as well as following the astronomical sowing and planting calendar.

What to do

Biodynamics is certified by Demeter (www.biodynamic.org.uk). This method of organic gardening has three main elements: using horn manure (BD 500) and horn silica (BD 501) as field sprays; using five herbal preparations, including yarrow, valerian and dandelion, on the compost heap; following a biodynamic calendar for planting and doing other jobs in the garden. Horn manure works in the root zone and horn silica is active in the area of light and plant growth.

You can make horn manure by filling a cow's horn with cow manure and burying it in the soil in autumn. Dig it up the following spring and dilute the manure at one teaspoon to 50 litres (11 gallons) of water. Alternatively, fill a 1m- (3ft-) deep, brick-lined 'cow-pat pit' in the garden with fresh cow manure that is treated with specially fermented compost preparations such as crushed egg and basalt dust. Cover the pit with a wet sack and wooden boards to keep out the weather. After three months, add a few grammes of the manure to 75 litres (16½ gallons) of water, stir, and use as a spray.

More options include packing camomile blossom in cow intestines or oak bark in animal skulls and burying them. There is not much scientific proof for these ideas, but working with the occult on your allotment may appeal if you are bored with the humdrum digging, planting, weeding and watering routine of gardening.

'A garden always has a point.'

Elizabeth Hoyt, *The Raven Prince*

Acknowledgments

The author would like to thank Helen Griffin and Becky Clarke at Frances Lincoln, Alys Fowler, Liz Dobbs, Jane Perrone, Joanna Fortnam, Marc Rosenberg and everyone else who has published his gardening writing, everyone at *Horticulture Week* and his family. He would also like to thank Bethan, William and Ted Appleby, Stephen Cookson, Paula Hignett, the RHS, and the Hattons and Merton Allotment Garden Association.

The publisher would like to thank the following copyright owners for permission to reproduce their images on the pages listed (l = left, r = right, t = top, b = bottom):

FOR PHOTOGRAPHS

Amateur Gardening 6. **Chris Cyprus** 12. **GAP Photos** 44tr Michael Howes; 137 Lynne Keddie. **Garden & Wood** 106. **Matthew Appleby** 32, 37, 89, 89, 102, 111, 120, 128, 128, 128, 146. **Shutterstock** 4 jordache; 10 Piotr Wawrzyniuk; 17 Durden Images; 18 Kelly Nelson; 22tl Simone Andress; 22tr Lithiumphoto; 22bl Iakov Filimonov; 22br courtyardpix; 24 StudioSmart; 26 dogi; 32 M. Cornelius; 32 chaoss; 32 Berna Namoglu; 37 Julia Reschke; 37 Zygimantas Cepaitis; 38 Richard Hamill; 44 Denis and Yulia Pogostins; 44br ARENA Creative; 52 Jodie Richelle; 54 Kati Molin; 60 Georgios Kollidas; 62 Viktoriya Field; 62 PhotographyByMK; 62 LianeM; 62 Tatiana Grozetskaya;

67 Michaels/Shutterstock.com; 68 RHIMAGE; 71 Scott L. Williams; 74 Simone van den Berg; 78 Maisna; 78 audaxl; 78 utoplec78; 78 Darren Baker; 84 Gladskikh Tatiana; 86 c.bya norman; 89 Tami Freed; 92 Calin Tatu; 97 Sandra Zuerlein; 98 Dirk Ott; 100 BMJ; 102 Iryna Art; 102 Julija Sapic; 102 Larina Natalia; 111 ChameleonsEye; 111 scigelova; 114 Gary L. Brew 117 mythja; 128 daseaford; 129 Botamochy; 130 gbphoto21; 1 Stargazer; 130 iwka; 130 Lilyana Vynogradova; 137 Cosmin Sa 143 Citi Jo; 144 Anton Petrus; 151 audaxl; 157 Dusan Zidar; 1 psv; 165 Irina1977; 165 joingate; 165 Katharina Wittfeld; 165 Hintau Aliaksei; 166 S.Cooper Digital; 181 luri; 184 iravgustin. **The Garden Collection** 126 Nichola Stocken Tomkins; 160 & 175 Andrew Lawson; 178 James Kerr. **Thinkstock:** Hemera 123 iStockphoto: 8, 31, 37, 40, 44bl, 46, 51, 57, 77, 83, 89, 112, 146 171, 172. Stockbyte: 2, 111, 152.

FOR ILLUSTRATIONS

Shutterstock 3Art 35; Aleks Melnik 2; bioraven 5, 65, 135; Devochka i zaicheg 154; Extezy 94; Hein Nouwens 14, 20, 119 lynea 72; Michele Paccione 43; Morphart Creation 1, 28, 58, 8 148; Nikiparonak 48, 105, 124; RetroClipArt 141.